The Energy of Expansion

Edited by Erica Glessing

Bonnie,
thank you for
having me on your
wonderful show!
It was such
a pleasure to
meet you!
♡ Ashley

Happy Publishing

The Energy of Expansion

Compiled and Edited by Erica Glessing

FIRST EDITION
978-0-9896332-0-8

Cover Design by Deborah Perdue,
www.IlluminationGraphics.com

Interior Design & Typography by
www.BookPublishingMentor.com

Published by Happy Publishing, www.HappyPublishing.net

The Energy of Expansion
Foreword by Katherine McIntosh

Expansion is the energy of receiving when you aren't trying to figure out the space you're in. Have you ever had a moment of total bliss? The world disappears and you become one with the molecules of the universe. Joy is not separate from who you are. Space is not separate from who you are. Expansion is not separate from who you are. Instead, these elements permeate the vibrational resonance of your being and elevate you into a state that is you. You are not separate from them. You are not separate from you, and every molecule that makes up who you are also makes up the molecules of the entire universe.

My definition of true expansion is the willingness to receive the awareness of everything around you all the time so that you are not defined by what happens to you, but instead you are invited to be the co-creator of possibilities, beyond what you previously imagined. You cannot think yourself into the greatness that you are. You expand into the space of your greatness and then receive all the molecules that want to support you and expand with you. The universe is waiting to contribute to you. You are greatness, beyond words.

My invitation for you is to read the words in this book from the space of BEING that when the universe disappears, you become one with the molecules, not from thought, but from the experience of receiving the energetic download of it. These words contain an energy that will invite you to go beyond the cognitive mind and into the space of your being that will elevate the frequency of your thoughts.

Have you ever had the experience of reading a book that while you read it, you knew your entire life was changing because of it? This is my invitation to you – to allow the words to be the catalyst that takes you on a journey like never before. I wonder who you'll be on the other side? Enjoy the journey.

Katherine McIntosh
www.KatherineMcIntosh.com

Table of Contents

Chapter 1

The MindBody Mechanics of Expansion
By Dr. Kimberly D'Eramo

How do you define health? Is it:

- not having a medical diagnosis?

- not being on any medications?

- being fit and at your ideal weight?

- the absence of disease?

I'm going to give you a new perspective of health that is more dynamic and includes the idea of "Expansion."

Early in my medical career, I was diagnosed with an obscure chronic illness doctors said would continue indefinitely and require medications to manage. With all I'd learned about the science of MindBody Medicine, I knew this was not the right answer for me. I learned about the body's ability to heal itself, and understood that we are involved in creating our health, or lack thereof. I knew I could initiate a change in my health....but how could I make this happen? Try as I did for months, I hadn't been able to make it happen.

When I received this grim diagnosis, I began avidly practicing MindBody Tools, and within 10 days I reversed the entire illness. My lab values returned to normal. I had my vibrant energy back and enjoyed exercise again. I no longer experienced constant pain in my back and joints...and haven't had a migraine headache since.

Over the next several years I studied MindBody Medicine even more intensely and applied it to my practice of clinical medicine. I have come to understand the reasons why my body became so ill. I've now learned how to reliably create vibrant health in my body, and have shared this will hundreds of thousands of patients.

The biggest reason I had become so ill and didn't get better −no matter what I did − was that I was so focused on wanting to get better. I wanted to "fix" the problem, and was unable to accept and embrace the state I was in. I literally fought my own body. This created tremendous resistance. I was resisting feeling bad and only wanted to feel good. This sounds reasonable enough, and is part of our natural survival instinct. However, when we are unable to move through the feelings of "Contraction" with ease and grace, we prevent ourselves from easily moving into Expansion.

To explain what expansion is, think of this:

Have you ever had a moment when everything was going wonderfully well and life just felt perfect? Your body felt great, your life was in order, you were in perfect timing, things were complete, you were enjoying what you were doing and life just felt wonderful.

Typically nothing monumental has happened before moments like these. You haven't won the lottery, found out you'll be starring in a hit film, or just met the love of your life. These moments happen in an ordinary day while you're just walking around, but for some reason, Life feels divine.

In moments like these, your body is in ideal health. Your hormones are balanced, brain activity is harmonious and clear, organ function is at its best, and you are detoxifying through every cell. This is a state of health where your MindBody unit is working the way it is meant to work. It has nothing to do with whether you have a diagnosis of diabetes, cancer, or depression...in these moments your body enters a state of vibrance.

Expansion doesn't occur because of anything outside of you, or because of a dramatic shift in your circumstances. It happens when things inside you align, and you experience the miracle of life without internal drama/trauma to cover it up. Life is not always like this. If it were, there would be no contrast to help you grow. Expansion is the process of being able to fully embrace and appreciate everything that's happening. Contraction is what prepares us to expand.

Expansion is more than having more in your life, being a better person, or growing in prosperity. It is a neuro-chemical physiologic state that is created in your body at the cellular level. This chemical state is either one that promotes health, or one that depletes health. I teach my patients to connect with their body and become adept at feeling whether they are in an "expanded" or "contracted" state. Awareness of this is one of the most valuable tools I can teach you. This alone is often enough to create an immediate shift in your entire system.

Expansion is when you feel a sense of health and vibrance. Your cells secrete chemicals that bring about wellbeing and increased energy. Expansion accelerates healing. It slows aging. There are hormones and antioxidants secreted by your body during expansion that repair DNA, and turn of gene expression for diseases like diabetes and cancer. During expansion, your body is better able to break down food, absorb nutrients, detoxify waste products, and eliminate what your body does not need. Expansion makes your body healthy, and your cells vibrant.

Contraction is the opposite. This occurs when you are not going with the flow. Contraction is a state when the body secretes chemicals that cause harm. Stress chemicals like cortisol, which are helpful for a short term, are harmful to the body when sustained long term. The stress state, or contracted state, has been shown to cause inflammation that underlies every major chronic illness known to man.

Autoimmune illness is an inflammatory disorder where the

immune system reacts against the body. Cancer stems from an inflammatory chemistry that causes cells to have accelerated growth and an abnormal lifecycle. Diabetes develops due to chronic inflammation that impairs sugar metabolism and damages cells. Heart disease occurs due to inflammation in the vessel wall that causes plaques to build up and block blood flow. Contraction not only feels bad. It makes you sick and eventually makes you die.

Expansion and contraction are more than just physical chemical states. They are the quality of energy that is emitted from your body. Research over the past decade has shown amazing things about the human body we never thought possible in the past. At our most basic level, our cells are made of molecules, which are made of atoms. Those atoms are made of subatomic parts, and the way these parts behave changes everything about the way we previously understood matter. Instead of being solid things that behave like particles, subatomic parts behave more like waves of energy. That means that instead of an electron being a solid thing that can be found at one place at one time, it's more like a field of energy that is present everywhere at the same time. All this science reveals that we aren't so solid after all. At our most basic level, we are an energy field.

Every energy field has an impact. So as we walk down the street, we not only walk *in* an energy field, we are an energy field. We carry with us our body of energy that has an impact on everything around us. That's how we create the life we live. We literally emit the cause for it.

When you are in an expanded state, you think thoughts of Joy, Love and Appreciation. Your cells secrete chemicals that make you healthy and thrive....your energy field emits this vibrant juice of Life....and it impacts everything around you. This reflects, strengthens and supports your state of vibrance and well-being.

When you feel contracted you think "I hate my life," "I'm worthless," or "I can't do it." Your cells respond accordingly by producing stress chemicals and inflammation. You feel emotionally down, frustrated, angry or anxious, and you emit energy that reflects this low-frequency state. Others around you feel bad because of this, and do not treat you in a loving way. Therefore, your stress state creates your experience of being abused, fired, shouted at, ignored, or judged.

This is a very basic description of what takes place in your body during Expansion and Contraction, but it serves us in helping you understand why it's so important to get a handle on consciously creating expansion in your body.

Your body is hard-wired for survival.

Your nervous system has automatic alarm systems in place to know when it is threatened, and to unconsciously direct you to back off even before you consciously register the danger. So you can understand why it can be so difficult to expand into security, love, abundance when your entire being is encased in a metaphorical suit of armor.

When I have patients who have been in abusive or stressful situations in their youth, it can be difficult for them to embrace the health and vibrance that is available to them as an adult. Even though they're in safe, secure, supportive surroundings, their brain and cellular communication will not carry that information. It's simply the way their nervous system has adapted. Unless they have the tools to repattern their system, there is no way for them to enter the world of abundant health. It's like being locked in a jail cell looking out at a peaceful pasture that you just can't play in. For people like this, even a safe world feels threatening.

How does this happen?

First of all, when you've had stress in early development, the body has increased receptors for stress hormones and a highly developed sense of danger. Triggers that might otherwise go unnoticed will initiate hyper-alertness and anxiety. Stress hormones like cortisol are secreted at higher than normal levels, and the body's glands and receptors have adapted to this. Nerve pathways have been established that carry this type of information over and over and over... so that something as subtle as a dog barking can instantaneously trigger a full blown stress response throughout every organ system in your body.

Neurons that fire together wire together.

Nerve conduction and neuronal networks are one of the key reasons that expansion takes work. Basically, your brain creates shortcuts to initiate the chemical-emotional states that you are in most often. This makes depression, anxiety, anger...or joy, ease, and abundance states of habit.

The more often you enter these states, the easier it is for your brain and body to enter them automatically. Eventually, something as simple as saying your child's name, instantaneously increases oxytocin, dopamine, and endorphins. This brings a sense of joy, love and bliss. Likewise, the very thought of your ex, or a memory of a past blunder can initiate an immediate feeling of dread and a pit in your stomach.

For many of us, the habitual states are stress states. Instead of the feeling of expansion, (love, joy, peace, enthusiasm) the brain signals contraction and ignites the fight-or-flight response. The fight-or-flight response is triggered by the sympathetic nervous system. It's the automatic, involuntary, chemical, neurologic, and hormonal signals that gear your body to take action and fight...or flee. There is a third option in this state where we freeze. If you have ever done any public speaking and been tongue-tied, you have experienced this response.

When I was in high school I was in a chronic state of stress, as you may identify with. There was discord between my parents that no one talked about, and I held my own thoughts that I was somehow inferior to everyone else. My stomach was in knots for at least a couple of years. Very embarrassingly, I would sometimes involuntarily pass gas. Yes, really. In high school!! It was awful beyond belief, and I remember one time it happened in the middle of class in the middle of a dead silence!

Just the idea of this memory still brings back that feeling of freezing with embarrassment, even though decades have passed since this incident. All I could do was pray to die. It makes me cringe to even think of this! I have no idea if anyone has ever felt so embarrassed in the history of the world, but I share this story to demonstrate the powerful triggers in the brain and cells that are associated with intense stress.

What happens when we are in this type of pattern? Cortisol and other stress hormones initiate changes in brain activity, blood flow and organ activity, and affect every function in your body. In the short term (the time it takes to out run a tiger) this is relatively harmless and is followed by a balancing of hormones, normalization of brain activity, and restoration of peace in the body. However, in the chronic state (which most people are living in most of the time) the fight-or-flight mechanism does not get turned off and this creates illness and disease at every level.

You would think it would be natural for our mind and body to embrace wellness, vitality, serenity, ease and abundance. After all, as human beings, this is our natural state and the state in which all of our organ systems function optimally. When we experience the chemical-emotional state of expansion, (also known as the "Relaxation Response," our hormones are balanced, our breathing is deep and full, our digestion is ideal, the brain activity is harmonious, and the kidneys function optimally. However, since our systems are primarily set up to survive, the stress response does kick in. At this point in society there are multiple triggers everywhere designed to ignite our stress response. We must repetitively intervene in order to retrain our nervous system and override its' memory.

If you've ever experienced something wonderful happening, then had a feeling of suspicion and doubt that it wouldn't last, i.e. the "waiting for the other shoe to drop" feeling, you have experienced your hard-wiring in action. It happens, for example, if you're used to men being rude and dismissive, then you meet a wonderful man who is kind, sweet, and loving. Your brain literally cannot adapt that quickly to new expanded information. It just won't accept that new information as "real," so you either can't embrace it ("Yeah, right!") or you embrace it, but later bump it out. This is one reason why some women are not interested in "nice guys." It just doesn't match their hard-wiring. It's more comfortable for us to go with what's familiar than to do the work of expanding into something new.

For example, I had a patient experience complete reversal of his chronic severe back pain in just one session with me, only to insist that this wasn't possible. He was a highly trained MD psychiatrist, and simply had no point of reference for how this could be possible. His system literally would not accept it. After calling the next day to tell me "It's amazing! I feel wonderful and have no pain for the first time in 10 years! I can't believe it," ...his pain returned within the week. On his follow up visit he asked me not to use the "strange" techniques I'd done with him the last visit explaining, "Let's just see if we can get some improvement doing things the regular way so I know it's real."

More often, my patients and course participants open up to the MindBody tools I teach, and successfully retrain their brain to receive new kinds of information. This can be seen in as short at eight weeks on a functional MRI of the brain. You don't have to wait for eight weeks to experience the effects, however. The chemical and cellular changes happen instantaneously.

The other day I was coming up the stairs entering my home after a day in the Emergency Room seeing patients. I was right on time, which is not typical for me, and I felt amazing. I had a bag of wonderful healthy food to cook for dinner and had the thought: "My life is perfect right now and I have everything I want." I literally witnessed my mind scanning my body and my life, and searching for a problem. "Certainly there's something here to worry about; my life's not perfect!" I laughed because it was days after Erica Glessing had asked me to be a part of this book, and I witnessed the process of expansion occurring in my body as I quieted down that thought, and just E-X-P-A-N-D-E-D into bliss!

It takes this kind of quieting to allow expansion. If I hadn't been already focusing my attention on the themes for this book, I might have missed what was happened or experienced something entirely different. You must stay present to create these changes so your default system doesn't just take over. There will be some level of resistance from your hard-wired patterns. After all, change is threatening to the established set of pathways! If it was comfortable and routine, it wouldn't be growth.

Expansion is moving into a new level of aliveness that is not your usual state, so by nature it's uncomfortable. You need to open and stretch to allow this process to occur. This brings up another point about your mind and body:

What you focus on, expands.

Your mind will bring to your consciousness the information that you tell your mind is pertinent. Since I had been mulling over the idea of expansion, my mind knew I wanted to be alerted to this process within myself. A great MindBody tool to use to activate this principle is "Asking Better Questions." Your mind loves to retrieve the information when you tell it what you want!

When patients ask "What's wrong with me?!" they think they will come up with an answer that gives them a solution. However, what they will continue to receive all the evidence of what's wrong. A better practice is to ask: "Why am I so healthy and strong?" I guarantee you will get information that serves your health!

In one of my online programs called Mind Your Body, I dedicate an entire section to upgrading your neurologic capacitance. That's the ability of your nervous system to carry information like health, love, harmony, joy and peace. I bring participants through specific MindBody tools that literally change the physical brain and allow it to conduct new types of information. With practice, studies have shown, the brain not only develops healthier structures, but it establishes neurologic signals that create a baseline of health and harmony. Basically, with practice, you can train your brain to embrace Health and Harmony. You can expand your brain!

How do you do this? Well, there are a few things to understand about the mind and body that will guide you through the process of expansion, and changing your brain.

The first point is: The Mind Loves Games!!! (Don't you?!) – so I create MindBody tools that make expansion fun and interesting. When something is framed as a game, it immediately brings the feeling of expansion! I had a game I used to play decades ago to bring myself a sense of expansion at school. Since I would occasionally become bored, lonely or depressed, I intuitively created this to immediately lift my mood and increase my energy. It kept me interested and engaged in a school system that was otherwise mundane and boring, and where I felt wrong. (I had no idea it had brain and health benefits at the time!) During the day as I went about my routine, I would bring my imaginary best friend to school with me in my mind. This person loved me, adored me, understood me, and I could tell her anything. It made my day fun and interesting, gave me a new perspective on things that would otherwise seem mundane, and provided an outlet for the commentary in my head that would otherwise go unexpressed.

Later in life this same tool was profoundly beneficial when I wanted to manifest a life-partner. I had been divorced. I had been in other relationships where I was not fully met. I had begun to feel as though I would never find someone to share my most intimate life with. However, I knew that the common denominator in these experiences was me! Somehow I needed to validate my experiences, give myself the compassion I needed, and create the changes that would have me find a partner I could share my life with.

Under the guidance of a coach, I wrote love letters to myself from my greatest lover (an excellent expansion exercise!!) and I also wrote love letters to my greatest lover from me. This allowed me to establish patterns in my brain for this type of communication and receiving of love and understanding at a level that was entirely new. It worked. Months later, to our surprise, my now husband and I came across the letters and he said: "This is exactly what I say to you!" It was true. The words, the emphatic encouragement, all the things I most needed to hear and wrote to myself for support, were the very same words he typically used with me.

Remembering to make expansion a game will serve you. The idea of "working on yourself" brings to mind a feeling of dread and focuses your attention on the problem. That's no fun and you won't stick with it. To generate real and lasting change, you must stick with the process until it becomes automatic, so make it fun!

The second point to remember is that The Mind Needs Specific Instructions. Esoteric ideas are interesting, but there isn't really anything to sink your teeth into. If there is no hard-core procedure, the brain just doesn't know what to do with the information, and no change happens. In fact, the more conceptual stuff you try to learn about expansion, the more likely you are to be frustrated that it's not working, and so you contract! When you do MindBody tools, there has to be a procedure so the brain has a reference point for beginning, middle, and end. This gives the mind context to know whether it has done things "right." The mind loves to be right, so use that to your advantage!

The third factor in expansion is that you must go beyond thinking about expansion and get into the Feeling of Expansion! The mind communicates in images, and the body translates those images into chemical signals. The chemical soup bathes every cell and creates your emotional state. In order to embody a new concept in your cells, you must create an emotional shift. You've got to feel the change! That means if you're thinking about the idea of abundance: having plenty of money, plenty of love, plenty of health...whatever – you have to go beyond understanding what abundance means, and have an experience of actual abundance.

Emotion is how your body manifests ideas. The concepts become real in your cells! That is how manifestation occurs. Your body creates the cellular reality of your thoughts. Your body is the first interface that your thoughts have in the physical world. Let the ideas you are expanding into materialize in the chemistry of your cells. You will feel it as your emotional state. Then you can choose whether this is really something you want to fully create. Something may sound like a good idea conceptually, but you will know whether it's a good idea by how it feels.

This leads to my last point: Expansion Feels Good! This seems simplistic to state, however, it's what most often trips people up when they're taking steps toward self-improvement. Teachings applied out of context can end up causing harm in your system. For example, my husband makes it a habit to study billionaires. Carlos Slim, Sir Richard Branson, Vinod Khosla, Bill Gates, Warren Buffett....etc. He has fun meeting them, or watching online videos and growing from their teachings. However, at one point he was contracted and stuck in his business. I could tell he was pushing things forward and not in the state of allowing Life to work things out. I encouraged him to "Let It Happen" instead of always trying to "Make It Happen," (which is interestingly the name of his business!) He immediately cited multiple comments from Bill Gates, Warren Buffet and others, who insist that action is needed and that you must be the creator of your dreams. While these points are true, they are not universal. What I mean is that there are times when these truths apply and serve you, and times when doing things this way actually works against you (as in this instance.) When used out of context, applying the teaching or advice causes more resistance in your body.

How do you tell the difference? Feel it in your body. When I asked him to feel into that urge to push, to force, to "Make It Happen" he just felt more contracted. Thankfully, he's evolved enough to know that this isn't the way to create success. He opened to the idea that there are forces of Life beyond what he could possibly see or know working things out, and that Life is on his side taking care of the details. It was okay for him to let go and allow things to sort out; to stop pushing and take what was coming his way. This thought felt better, so he went with it. In a few moments of embracing this ease, his mind opened, he laughed, and he remembered that the whole point of what he's creating in his business is Joy. He said "If there isn't Joy, I don't want this to work out anyway."

The point is, anytime you are evaluating an idea or a truth, it must *feel good in your body* if it's going to move you into expansion. Trust your body! It has wisdom beyond anything you can imagine. There is far more about the mind and body that we *don't* know than all the millions of volumes of medical journals and text that we *do* know. In fact, what we've discovered about the brain in the last five to 10 years is greater than everything we've discovered about the brain in all of human history before that time! Think about that. That means the entire foundation of our scientific and medical system neglects almost all of what we now know about the capacity of the mind.

With all this said, you can leave it up to your body to create change and heal your life. I'm going to share with you my favorite MindBody tool to create expansion. You can use it anytime during your day, although at first it will take setting aside a minute or two to learn and integrate the process. Once you've done that, you'll use this tool while you're driving your car, making dinner, talking with your spouse, or writing a book!

The tool can be found at bit.ly/ExpansionTool, so go now for the awesome video!

"The Instant Elevation Technique."

The steps are: A-B-C.

A. Become AWARE of how you are feeling in your body:

- **Sense what's happening in your body** on every level: physically, mentally, and emotionally.

- **Rate this on a scale of 1-10,** with 10 being the best.

Becoming aware of what's going on in your body increases your brains ability to pay attention to this kind of information. With practice, part of your attention will constantly be in your body, attentive to what's going on. You are literally developing new and strengthened neurologic connections in your body and brain that deliver this information.

- **Set your alarm** to go off 3 times daily to practice.

B. BREATHE slowly and deeply 3 times:

- **Relax your shoulders and let the breath come all the way into your belly,** ballooning out your belly with the inhale. Let your belly come back in with a long, slow exhale.

This turns of the fight-or-flight breathing pattern and establishes the "relaxation response" which has been heavily documented to reverse disease. This breathing changes activity in the brain so you become aware of more expanded information, and deactivate the parts that trigger stress.

- **Do this every time you become aware** that you are feeling bad or anxious in any way. In just 3 breaths you will feel a sense of calm, clarity and relaxation. It also decreases pain.

C. CHOOSE to expand:

- **State aloud or to yourself** *"I choose to be well and at peace now,"* **or** *"I choose to relax and let my body heal."*

You are consciously putting new information into your system.

By doing steps A and B, you have set the stage to communicate to your cells and repattern your brain. This is the time when visualization, affirmations and other MindBody tools will have immediate and powerful impact!

Practice this "A-B-C" sequence several times daily as an expansion exercise. Use it any time you notice you are contracted, and want to effect a change in your body or in the circumstances of your life.

Coming into an expanded state means your cells immediately stop secreting damaging stress chemicals and start the process of healing. This impact goes far beyond your cells. Your energy field has been measured up to 8-10 feet beyond your physical body, and it correlates with your emotions. That means your emotional state impacts others around you energetically. You literally create the results in your life through your energy, and your emotions are the key to knowing what your energetic state is.

Continue to keep your *attention* in your body, and your *intention* on expanding, so you retrain your brain, rewire your body, and become a generator of a Joyful, Peaceful, Blissful world. I wish you a life beyond your wildest dreams and would love to support you in any way I may.

ABOUT THE AUTHOR: KIMBERLY D'ERAMO

Kimberly D'Eramo, D.O. is a board-certified Emergency Medicine physician, speaker, TV personality, bestselling author, and founder of the American Institute of Mind-Body Medicine. Dr. D'Eramo empowers patients to instantly increase energy, enhance productivity, and reverse disease. Be sure to claim your free "Instant Elevation Technique" to expand now at: bit.ly/ExpansionTool.

Chapter 2

Living an Empowered, Expansive Existence
By Dr. Lisa Cooney, LMFT

When I was seven, I stood looking out my bedroom window at the moon with a prayer heavy on my heart.

I vowed that one day I would find a way beyond the life that I was living. I vowed that I would do what it took to create a world where all children could lay their head on their pillows at night and rest peacefully.

While I was only seven, I had already experienced all kinds of physical, sexual, emotional and mental abuse that continued well into my 20s. At that young age I committed my life to getting myself out of what I call the invisible cage of abuse because I knew something else was possible.

It took me decades, a lot of support and a lot of courage to arrive at a place in my life where I am an embodiment of the energy of expansion. I have become a leading authority on thriving after childhood sexual abuse. I have supported thousands of people in living beyond their own abuse to create limitless lives.

I travel the world facilitating classes. I have a radio show on Voice America where I reach thousands of listeners every week with my show, "Beyond Abuse, Beyond Therapy, Beyond Anything." I have a beautiful sanctuary of a home in California where I live with my enjoyable other.

You could say I kept my promise to that little seven-year-old me. I chose to never give up, never give in and always go for what else was infinitely possible. I am doing everything I can to eradicate and eliminate abuse off this planet so that more children and more adults live the empowered, expansive existence that is their birthright.

Whether or not you experienced abuse as a child, you may be locked in your own invisible cage that keeps you from being the energy of expansion and the greatness you desire. You, like me, may have also vowed to yourself to do what it takes to create the world you know is possible. Yet you're just not sure how to do this.

Or perhaps you forgot you vowed to do this and here is your wake up call to action!

I invite you on a journey - together let's explore the ways the "invisible cage" has kept you from your greatness so that you, too, can move beyond the constriction of the cage and into an embodiment of the energy of expansion.

So what is the energy of expansion? If you're going on this journey it helps to know what you are seeking to create!

The Energy of Expansion is...

• Knowing your greatness and the magical being you truly be

• Living a life of fun, freedom, joy and radical aliveness

• Recognizing there are infinite possibilities always

• Asking for and receiving that which you desire

• Experiencing communion with yourself and others

• Gifting that which is uniquely yours to the world

• Choosing to create an empowered life beyond any limits

Now imagine what kind of life you can create when you embody the energy of expansion...

Pretty fantastic, isn't it?!

So let's look at three of the biggest limitations of the invisible cage and how to move beyond them to embody the energy of expansion you truly be.

From Victimization to Empowerment

As a child I became pretty shut down. Nothing I did made a difference: I still got abused. I grew up believing there was nothing I could do to escape abuse. I was a victim to it.

I carried this victim story into my 20s. I drank, partied, did drugs and engaged in other reckless behavior to try and escape the pain of my past abuse. I didn't care about myself.

It took a conversation with my Family Violence professor in undergraduate school to realize I wasn't worthless. She helped me see how common it is for children who have been abused to believe they are bad and wrong.

This professor was the first person who ever asked me if I was ok. Her act of kindness flooded me with the awareness of how *not* ok I was. She helped me see that there was something I could do to overcome my past abuse and be more than ok one day.

As though handed a key, I began to unlock myself from the cage of my own abuse. I quickly saw how I had been repeating the pattern of abuse against myself through my reckless behavior. I committed to choosing new behaviors that weren't destructive.

I also realized that I wasn't able to stop this pattern completely on my own. I sought out professional support and through those confidential conversations I released the victim story I had been living for almost three decades.

This journey beyond the victim story led me through the invisible cage to me and ultimately ***out of the cage*** to who I truly be! I discovered who I actually was beyond the shut down miserable self-destructive girl. I learned I was kind, brilliant, phenomenal and funny.

I also realized I had other choices for how I lived and how I related to myself and others. As I exercised new choices I grew more confident. The old patterns of abuse no longer had power over me. I now had the power over my abuse. I had the power to choose a new life for myself.

What about you? Is the "victim-story" ruling your life?

Have you been repeating the abuse cycle through self-destructive patterns too, like I was? (Do you get how disempowering this actually is?)

What if you can actually create your life from choice rather than destruction?

If you experienced any form of abuse in your life, or any kind of "wrongness," you may be more committed to the victim story rather than the possibility of life beyond it. You may feel like a victim to circumstance, and like I felt for so long, like there is nothing you can do to change it.

May my story awaken you to *NOT* hang onto the victim story any longer! If you've chosen it, let it be a "phase" in your journey from the invisible cage to the energy of expansion.

Are you ready to let go of the victim story?

Here are three steps to move beyond victimization and into empowerment:

1. Get support from a professional

• Often times the same people you share your issues with are the people – family or friends – who helped create those issues.

• Talking with an expert accelerates your own movement in the journey out of victimization.

2. Share your story and release all your secrets

• Secrets keep you in the role of victim; they create shame and keep you disempowered and stuck in constriction and limitation.

3. Choose to let go of – and move beyond - the "victim story"

- When you let go of your story and move beyond it you begin to step into being the magic you truly be. You discover the energy of expansion available to you beyond the cage.

As you move beyond your victim story you'll begin to experience the energy of expansion: freedom, joy and your own greatness. You'll begin to see more possibilities for yourself and your life.

And you'll discover new sources of your own potency in surprising places...

From Armoring to Vulnerability

When my mom swore at me and called me names I didn't cry or let on how upset I was. I just did what was asked, got it over with and went to my room to hide.

When my mom beat me I 'steeled up' and braced myself. I knew not to cry because then she would hit me harder. If I just took it from her and put on my invisible "armor" by not crying I knew it would be over sooner.

I grew up believing that I was safer if I was tough. I developed really thick armor to protect my soft insides. This way my abusers only got my armor; they never fully "got" me.

I call this armoring the "invisible porcupine phenomenon." *(I dedicated two entire radio shows to this topic – you can find the free recordings of these shows on my website).*

Just like a porcupine defends itself with sharp quills, you too might be wearing armor made of invisible quills. This is your best attempt to protect yourself from a world that doesn't seem safe.

How expansive can you be when you're constantly defending yourself?

Just like you hoped the quills would keep an abuser away, they now keep relationships, money, clients and all else at a "safe" distance. These quills block you from receiving the life you desire because it feels dangerous to receive anything.

How much are you uninviting into your life now with these quills?

And just like the quills of the invisible porcupine point outwards and keep everything in life (relationship, money, clients, etc.) at a "safe" distance, they also point inwards and keep you from coming forward into your own life.

At some point, perhaps a long time ago, you learned it wasn't "safe" to come forward. In your attempt to escape your abuse, or tell someone about your abuse, you may have disconnected or dissociated. Either way, you went away from yourself to try to keep yourself safe.

So you keep poking yourself with your own quills in the form of judgments and the story that it's not safe to be you. You keep yourself small, perhaps even invisible, to try and escape any perceived danger that may still be "out there."

Want to know the most painful thing about this?

You're living your own life at an "armored and safe" distance from yourself, never fully receiving the beauty and potency of YOU. In this way, you are never experiencing the strength of your vulnerability.

Vulnerability is being YOU without the armor, without the defenses.

It took me being in relationship with therapists, healers, partners and ultimately, myself, to trust that I could be "safe" if I removed my armor. Yet over time I finally did release both my inner and outer quills.

As my quills dissolved I discovered a new level of vulnerability. In this soft open space I experienced communion with myself and others like I had never known before. I was able to ask for and receive what I truly desired. And I felt more alive than ever before because I was finally receiving myself and my life fully!

I discovered a potency in my vulnerability that looked and felt a whole lot different from the strength of my "steeling up." This potency is the best "protection" you could ever truly require.

Are you ready to lay down the armor and experience the potency of your own vulnerability?

When the armor is gone you may feel a little "naked" or overexposed. Please know this is normal – nothing is wrong! It's just your soft inner space becoming more exposed to a life of communion with yourself beyond the armor.

Yet there is one final pervasive aspect of the invisible cage that will block you from the energy of expansion unless you learn how to move beyond it...

From Judgment to Kindness

Judgment is the opposite of expansion. It is constriction, limitation, and a pervasive form of self-abuse. Judgment is the real epidemic of our reality.

When you judge another you're actually defending, disconnecting, denying and dissociating from what you are not willing to see about yourself. Judgment keeps you lying to you and locks you back into the invisible cage of abuse. This keeps you locked away from you, from others, from living and certainly from creating the life you desire.

When you judge yourself, you become your own eternal jailer and further lock yourself into the wrongness of you. Judgment returns you to the comfort of what you know (how "bad" you are) and guarantees that you never have to be more than you are right now. It solidifies the invisible cage of abuse.

Judgment keeps you small and struggling, victim-y and pow-
erless, armored and numb. As a result, you stop generating
and creating beyond the cage; you're perpetrating you and
keeping the abuse cycle going.

How is this a kindness to you? Or anyone?

The only way to get beyond the cage and into the energy of
expansion is to get beyond judgment. So how do you do this?

**Here are steps you can take to access a space of no
judgment:**

Sit in a quiet space, close your eyes, and take a few deep breaths
Expand your energy into the earth

Offer your judgments to the earth as a contribution

1. Open up to receive the contribution the earth can be for you

2. Bring your energy back into yourself without your judgments

3. Notice what you're aware of

The earth is the one place where judgment can't reside. It's
the place you can return to again and again to release your
judgments and feel the peace and possibilities of expansion.

It's actually a kindness to gift your judgments to the earth.
By gifting the manure of judgment to the earth you fertilize

a new possibility for yourself and everyone else.

In the space of no judgment is kindness. Kindness is the truth of who you be and what you have always been.

Kindness is a generative energy. I have discovered after traveling the world and working with thousands of people that kindness is what is required to move beyond judgment, beyond abuse and beyond limitation. This generative energy is what creates a new life filled with the energy of expansion.

What would occur in 50 years on this planet if you chose kindness?

What would occur if you released the victim story and chose the path of empowerment?

What would occur if you released the armor and chose the potency of vulnerability?

Would disease disappear?

Would conflict ease?

Would you be happy?

How would the energy of expansion open you up to a world of new possibilities?

I remember my seven-year-old self staring at the moon,

dreaming of a life beyond abuse. Together we are creating this new world as we move beyond the cage of limitation and into the energy of expansion.

I thank you for expanding as the energy you be, because that will eliminate and eradicate all forms of abuse off this planet. I thank you for being the kind, vulnerable, empowered and potent being you truly be! Viva the energy of expansion! You are it. Be it!

ABOUT THE AUTHOR: DR. LISA COONEY LMFT

 Dr. Lisa Cooney is a leading authority on thriving after childhood sexual abuse. She is a licensed Marriage and Family Therapist, certified Access Consciousness ® Facilitator, Master Theta Healer and author in the books *The Energy of Happiness*, *The Energy of Receiving*, and of the upcoming books, *Kick Abuse in the Caboose: The Bridge to Radical Aliveness* and *When Did You Become a Slave to Abuse: Getting Free in a New Way.*

She has supported thousands of people over the past 20 years move beyond their abuse to create infinite possibilities for themselves and joyful lives. Find her at www.DrLisaCooney.com.

Chapter 3

Can Being "Too Sensitive" Make Me Sick?

By Ashley Stamatinos

Being an empath, or highly sensitive person, has been the greatest gift and the greatest challenge in my life. Has anyone ever labeled you as "too emotional" or "overly sensitive"? What if your sensitivity was actually a strength of yours and you just hadn't yet uncovered its full potential?

For me, being highly empathic used to mean that I was constantly anxious about the possibility of picking up other people's problems, thoughts, feelings, or issues of any kind. I felt as though even non-contagious illnesses could rub off on me, and I frequently experienced burnout from the constant overstimulation of my senses. Before I had the tools to use my sensitivities to my benefit, I struggled to find inner peace.

An empath is a person who is capable of feeling the emotions of others despite the fact that she is not actually going through the same situation. An empath often takes on the thoughts, feelings, sensations, and emotions of those around her. If you're not aware that you're empathic you may think those thoughts or pains are your own when you have actually picked them up from someone else.

As an empath, you experience the world around you in a different way than your peers. Sometimes smells, sounds, and light can be too much to handle. Your senses can get easily overwhelmed.

If a friend is distraught, do you start feeling it too? Do you find that your feelings are easily hurt? Do you shut down when you're in big crowds? Is feeling burnt out a normal reality for you? Do you prefer taking your own car places so that you can leave anytime? Is overeating or drinking something you find yourself doing to cope with emotional stress? If you can relate to most of these scenarios, then you are most likely an empath too.

Because I too am empathic, and I've spent over a decade developing this skill, I am highly tuned into my intuition. Some of the extremes I experience as an empath include speaking with the spirits of people and animals who have crossed over. My sense of smell can be so heightened that I can smell bacteria in someone's body, and I can smell when someone is dying. I use my sensitivity to know when people are lying and to know who needs me at any given moment. I am telepathic with my child and with the animals around me. I can see the energy fields of people and animals, and I use that information to determine where there are bodily imbalances. Being empathic also allows me to be very tuned into what people require of me at all times, and I am able to connect on a deeper level with others at a faster pace because of this. Most empaths are also natural healers, and I've used this gift of healing to channel energy to countless people with measurable results.

This awareness is positive in all the ways I've just described, but it's easy to take on other people's feelings and interpret them as our own. This can be quite painful for many empaths, and I know it was a huge source of suffering for me for years.

I realized I was a highly empathic person when I was in middle school and my mother would tell me I was trying to heal and help all my friends. My friends treated me like I was their psychologist and always came to me for suggestions. She would remind me that I needed to care for myself first instead of putting my friend's needs before my own.

For many years, the friendships in my life were not balanced. I was there for my friends whenever they needed something, but they were incapable of being there for me. I was giving so much, and they were giving very little. I found it terribly draining but didn't know how to change this cycle because I enjoyed being helpful and making such an impact in their lives.

People I didn't know would come up to me and tell me their whole life story. Random people trusted me with their deepest secrets only moments after meeting me.

I have always been very sensitive about cruelty to animals and children. Ever since I was young, I have been involved with rescuing animals. In my 20s, my husband and I became foster parents for sick baby kittens. We took in the sickest cats the shelter had, and we nursed them back to health. Over the years we took care of over 100 cats, and to this day it is still one of the most rewarding experiences I've ever had. It gave us so much pleasure to heal those little kittens that came into our home so sick, and they would leave healthy and happy to be placed into their forever homes.

From Sickness to Health

I moved to New York City to pursue a performing arts career just days before the 9/11 events. Shortly after 9/11, I developed fibromyalgia, chronic fatigue, and chronic pain. I also had terrible asthma while living in NYC. These challenging health issues put my dreams of a dancing career to an early end and forced me to really turn my focus inward to get healthy.

In my efforts to mend my body, I saw many different doctors that couldn't find anything wrong with me. I was put on epileptic seizure medications, muscle relaxers, and much more. I quickly realized that I was getting worse, not better. It didn't seem like all the medications were the best way for me to recover. I felt depressed and hopeless as the doctors were giving up on me one by one. I hit rock bottom. I was so sick at times that I felt like I was dying.

I spent two weeks in a pain rehab clinic after the pain got so bad it barely allowed me to get around. I would sleep 12 hours a night, exhausted from fighting the pain all day, every day. Luckily I had an incredibly supportive family, and they encouraged me to look into alternative methods to heal instead of continuing to mask the symptoms with western medications.

After trying many different natural healing techniques, I found daily energy treatments made a drastic difference. I combined daily energy treatments, acupuncture and herbal supplements with a change in my mindset and I regained my balance. That was my formula for success. I know each of us has a different formula for healing since we are each so unique, and my formula was exactly what I needed to get better.

I really put in the work, and I started to get better fast! I knew I was on to something, and I was finally getting a glimpse of the light at the end of the tunnel. I continued to get treatment in the holistic world, and now I no longer have any of the chronic symptoms I once had! Doctors can't explain my recovery because fibromyalgia usually gets worse, not better.

I once had a medicine cabinet full of pills, and I'm living completely free of them now. I haven't needed any western medications for many years now, and I am able to live a fully active life, pain free.

The Extremes of Empathy

When I was in college, I would try to go out with my friends to bars and clubs and sometimes found myself frozen, almost paralyzed. I had trouble talking or moving or even speaking. I felt like no one could possibly understand what was going on, so I tried not to tell anyone what I was experiencing.

Now I hear more and more empaths tell me they can relate to this kind of total shut down from extreme overstimulation. When this would happen, I felt like what I was experiencing was too extreme for others to understand. I didn't yet know that what I was experiencing was very typical for an empath.

About 20 percent of empaths are introverts, and 80 percent are extroverts. It's much easier to spot an introverted empath. I'm very extroverted, so most people don't guess how empathic I am if they don't know much about me. I'm a very charismatic, social person. Most people who are highly empathic find social settings to be painfully uncomfortable most of the time. One of the biggest reasons for this is that, without the necessary tools, they become emotional sponges and are constantly dumped on by those around them.

When you put me in an atmosphere with lots of people who are on drugs or drunk, I can feel them so intensely that, in the past, it overwhelmed me so deeply I could barely function. You can actually energetically get drugged or drunk when around entities or people that are drugged or drunk. If you too have experienced this, it is real...you're not making it up. It's happened to me at least five times, and it's one of the most uncomfortable things I've ever experienced.

It was like I was stoned or on drugs even though I hadn't taken anything. That's what can happen if you are an empath with hypersensitivity. It's actually pretty typical for highly empathic people to feel terrible in very crowded places, especially where there are people drinking or doing drugs.

I have also met many people who were reluctant to admit that they actually felt fearful of being near a person with a disease, whether it was contagious or not, because they felt they could contract it simply by being near the sick person. It's typical for highly sensitive people to become aware of the "symptoms" of those around them, and if they don't have the awareness that those symptoms don't belong to them, it can feel as though they do. This can increase and grow into a problem.

Awareness is key. Now that you know it's possible to experience this kind if extreme sensitivity, you'll be able to recognize what's going on right away and remove it before it causes you further discomfort.

Basically, being empathic is having a level of sensitivity that far exceeds most people. Empaths notice and pick up on subtleties that most people don't.

Not all empaths experience such extremes as I'm illustrating, so if you can relate to some of the more subtle examples but not the more intense ones, you are still an empath. There are varying degrees of empathy.

Uncovering What Does Not Belong to You

Whenever you have a body sensation, any thought in your head, any emotion, any belief, any fears or worries, ask yourself if that is yours or someone else's. Most of the time, the things you're experiencing don't belong to you; they are simply an awareness you're having about something someone else is experiencing. When you get the awareness that that thought, emotion, belief, or sensation isn't yours, you'll want to release it. To let it go, just say "return to source," or imagine it leaving you and going back to wherever you picked it up. It doesn't have to be more complicated than that. By saying "return to source," you have energetically let go of what you picked up. There is no need to hold onto other people's stuff. It's not helping them for you to process it for them. We all need to process our own things, so let it go and free yourself from that heaviness. It doesn't even matter if you know where you picked up the sensation or emotion that doesn't belong to you, so don't get stuck on trying to pin point where it originated. The point of origin doesn't matter. What matters is that you become aware that it doesn't belong to you, and you let go of it.

This tool was very instrumental for me when I started healing from my chronic pain, fibromyalgia, and chronic fatigue. While I was going through the worst parts of these challenges right after 9/11, I didn't immediately learn that most of the thoughts, emotions, and sensations in our body do not originate from us. When I finally realized this, I started getting the awareness that almost all of my pain and suffering was directly picked up from the people who were involved in the trauma surrounding 9/11.

My body was trying to heal them and help them by taking it on as my own. No wonder I was so miserable and in so much pain for those years!

If you are reading this and you are realizing you too had incredible pains and issues with your body or your life starting around September 2011, know that being an empath doesn't mean you need to be in close proximity to "ground zero." You can feel the trauma of a natural disaster or terrorist attack, for example, from anywhere in the world. That's one of our gifts and challenges.

As long as we immediately ask ourselves if the sensation, pain, or thought is ours, we will get better and better at not taking on other people's pains, and, rather, we will realize it's not ours before it embeds itself into us and starts to look like it is.

Your new awareness of how much you're holding onto that's not yours will allow you to step into a new way of functioning where you are no longer affected by everything going on around you. You'll become the captain of your ship instead of the passenger.

Now that I am constantly looking at my thoughts, emotions, and sensations and constantly asking the question "did this originate from me," I have an incredible awareness that allows me to stop suffering from other people's stuff.

It can be challenging for those who are empathic and don't have the tools or skills to use this as a gift. I find many people want to make it go away; they want to turn down their sensitivity. Many people conclude that being an empath is uncomfortable and that it causes more discomfort than ease. I know what that's like because I've been there.

Turning down your sensitivities isn't going to bring you more ease. Suppressing your empath abilities will only cause you more challenges.

What You Resist will Persist

It was Carl Jung who first said "What you resist persists," and many teachers have expanded on that by going on to say: "What you resist persists...and what you accept changes." I know this to be true from my own personal experience and from watching those around me professionally and personally.

When you resist your natural sensitivities you are actually

going to create more discomfort, so start asking yourself "what can my sensitivities do to contribute to my life?" and "how can I use my sensitivities to my advantage?"

Those who resist being empaths have the hardest time coping, and those who embrace being sensitive find the most ease in their lives.

I hear so many of you tell me over and over again how you are using innumerable tactics to protect yourselves and seeing minimal results. Have you felt like you are trying with all your might to stop getting your energy drained and your feelings hurt and it just keeps getting worse? The key is to stop protecting and resisting, and start function from allowance and surrender by lowering your walls and defenses.

This was a difficult concept for me to fully understand for about a year. It might take you a while to play around with this and work with it before you really get into the flow of not resisting.

To resist means to oppose, or push against, so when you put your focus on fighting or struggling against an unwanted situation in your life, like not making enough money, not being as healthy as you'd like, the loss of a loved one, or even separating from a romantic partner, what you are actually doing is attracting more of that lack of money, ill-health, relationship drama, and so on.

You won't get anywhere that you really want to be by resisting the unwanted, as all your attention is on the thing that you DO NOT want.

Stop Limiting Yourself

I no longer get burnt out and depressed, and I used to perpetually function from that space of depression and burn out. It's such a relief to be a highly functioning empath. I am actually working more and sleeping less, as I can maintain a high energy level consistently now. This is beyond what I thought was possible for myself.

If you're in a situation in your life where it seems like you keep spinning your wheels, and it seems like there is little hope for change, then please look at my story and allow it to give you hope. When the doctors told me "this is how it is, you can't heal this, only treat the symptoms," that was incredibly limiting, and I searched for a new possibility. I didn't allow their limiting beliefs to stop me from creating the change I desired, which was to attain health and happiness.

Has anyone ever limited you by telling you "this is just how it is," or maybe you have said that to yourself from time to time? Eliminate that phrase from your vocabulary. Every time you find yourself or someone else saying "this is how it is," replace that phrase with a question like "what else can I choose here?"

As I accepted being an empath, I gained a greater understanding of why I function the way I do, and it allows me to get out of resistance mode and into being in total allowance of my true nature.

I remember the moment that I stopped fighting my true nature was when the real healing began. I am now happier and healthier than ever and things in my life have been improving on every level ever since I made the choice to embrace my sensitivities as my greatest gift.

ABOUT THE AUTHOR: ASHLEY STAMATINOS

Ashley is widely known as the Empath Expert for her extensive work with highly sensitive adults and children. Her mission is to empower you to use your sensitivity as your greatest strength.

Ashley is the founder of Omorfi Healing, a business that she created as a platform to offer holistic education and healing to the world. She is passionate about teaching, and has been teaching for the last 10+ years. Many of her students have said that Ashley teaches with great patience and enthusiasm.

Within her practice she offers both online and in-person courses to those seeking a life they love. Her in-person courses are primarily available within the Chicagoland area at the premier energy education centers.

While Ashley's main focus within her practice is supporting highly sensitive people, she also has many other courses available for you. She teaches on a variety of topics. Some of the courses she teaches include:

How to Communicate with Spirits, A new Perspective on Parenting Intuitive Children, Empowering Holistic Teachers, Ignite Your Holistic Practice, Seeing and Knowing The Bioenergetic Field, Empowering The Empath and Powering Up Empathic Kids to list a few.

Ashley had just moved to NYC days before 9/11, and shortly thereafter she developed severe fibromyalgia, chronic fatigue, chronic pain and a piercing lung infection.

As a result, she was placed on powerful medications (including epileptic seizure medication) for years until she reached rock bottom. It came to a point where she was so sick that she felt like she was dying. Unfortunately, western medications were not helping, so she started exploring other avenues of treatment when she stumbled upon alternative modalities of treatment.

Immediately, there was a shift and a transformation that was occurring within Ashley. Her health started to improve rapidly to the shock of her doctors. As her journey of personal healing took off like a rocket, she began to see the world in a different light. Finally, she was able to feel relief and realize what it truly meant to live a fulfilling life.

Because of her personal healing experience, it led her to her calling of teaching holistic wellness and empowerment courses.

Miraculously, Ashley has eliminated all symptoms and leads a very different life now. One that is full of purpose, passion and optimum health in all areas of life.

She feels her real "credentials" have come from personally overcoming and conquering these health battles. Now, Ashley openly shares her recipe for healing the incurable from her unique perspective about overcoming life's obstacles.

A great way to stay in touch with Ashley is to join her Facebook community. Go to Facebook.com/OmorfiHealing and like her page where she regularly gives personal updates and shares what's new in the field. Check out Ashley TV on her YouTube channel by going to YouTube.com/OmorfiHealing. There you will see her regular posts including guided meditations, how-to videos and recordings of lectures and classes.

Are you wondering if you're Empathic? There is a free quiz she created for you available by visiting her website. After you take the test, you'll get detailed results to help you understand how empathic you are. You'll find the Empath Quiz is available on the home page of www.OmorfiHealing.com along with lots of other free videos and audio downloads. If you'd like to read more articles from Ashley, she has a blog that covers a variety of different topics. Check it out by visiting www.Omorfihealing.com and be sure to comment.

You can also get onto Ashley's mailing list, where you'll receive monthly tools and tips on creating an empowered life you love. She shares insights and freebies within this mailing list that are not offered anywhere else, so be sure to get on the list by signing up on the home page of www.OmorfiHealing.com.

Private one-on-one phone sessions are also available for you. You can go to her website and click on Private Sessions to get all of the details. Ashley does travel to guest lecture, and teach her specialty classes. If you'd like her to come to your business to teach a course or to give a guest lecture, please email info@omorfihealing.com for further information.

Chapter 4

The Living Possibility of You

By Melanie Clampit

Have you always known there was something else possible, a different way to be in the world, a different world that should be available for you to choose?

I'd like you to know that you are correct, and you are not alone. For most of my life I felt as if I were from somewhere else, as if I did not fit in. I never met people who could see what I saw or knew the possibilities I was aware of. I spent most of my teen and adult life searching for how to belong, how to fit in, and how make myself functional in this reality – but it never worked. After finally letting go of the need to fit in, it has become invaluable to create the world that I know is possible, for me and for others who also are aware of this – a world of magic, choice, possibilities, communion, and happiness.

This chapter is for you who seek what cannot be explained but that something that pulls you forward and has never let you give up. This is for you who may never have felt like you belonged here or fit in to the reality around you. This is for you who may have given up or forgotten the magic and miracle you are as I will show you that you can indeed exist here. For those of you who have been wanting to go or longing for "home", I invite you to create home here. It is possible, and I am living that possibility, and I invite you to a new reality.

I'd like to share with you an experience from my life that opened a door that sparked a question and desire in my universe that has led me to the life I always dreamed possible, and here to these pages, to you.

I'd like to take a moment with you here for you to get a sense of your body and the space you are right now. Close your eyes, take a breath, and just notice the lightness or heaviness in and around your body. Just notice, don't try to change it or judge it. We are just creating a point of awareness we will return to later. Thank you.

So where do I begin? Let's begin with a miracle.

In 2003 I attended a transformational workshop called "Creating Reality from your Dreams" in Sedona, Arizona, USA. During this retreat I made a demand of myself and stated in front of the participants, "I now choose to be me, anywhere, and with anyone," and as usual in my world, the universe, provided me with the gift of stepping into my new choice within a few hours.

About halfway through my short flight home to San Francisco, California, the flight attendant's voice come over the intercom asking if there was a doctor on board and to please come to the front of the plane. I was sitting at the back of the plane so I was watching to see if anyone responded and went up, no one did. I waited until they asked one more time and there was still no response from any passengers.

I was on the edge of my seat and had a deep desire to get up and go put my hands on whoever was up there. My inner dialogue went something like this:

"Get up and go put your hands on that person."
"WHAT?! No way, me? What can I do? I just took a Reiki class two weeks ago and I have no idea what I'm doing. Not me, no way."

"Get up and go put your hands on that person, do what you can do. Be yourself anywhere, and with anyone, remember?"

Apparently as I had this conversation with myself my body had edged its way forward nearly off of my seat and the woman next to me asked, "Miss, do you need to get up?"

"No. Well, maybe," I said. "They called for a doctor and no one has responded. I just learned hands-on healing and I have the awareness to put my hands on the person, but..."

"Then you should," she said and stood up.

Oh my God. That was not the response I was expecting!

I moved past her and stood in the aisle. My mind went blank and I began to walk. One step at a time, one foot in front of the other, only able to see the red dashes flashing past my feet as they moved me towards a future totally undefined and unknown. There was an older African-American woman in the very first seat of the front row of the plane slumped over, unconscious and three confused flight attendants who had no idea what to do about this situation.

I stopped at the male flight attendant and bent over the woman.

"Excuse me, I do a hands-on healing modality that might help. May I put my hands on this woman?"

He looked at me uncertainly and told me to go ask the woman flight attendant on the phone with a emergency worker trying to figure out what to do and what might be happening with this woman.

I said the same to her.

"Oh, everything is just fine. We have it all under control. Go on back to your seat. Thank you."

I turned and walked back to the man in front of the woman, still unconscious.

Like hell I was gonna go back to my seat! I just made the longest hardest walk of my life so far that took all of my courage and I was absolutely not walking back now.

I stopped at the male flight attendant again, and repeated that I might be able to assist.

He was looking quite desperate at this point, stood back, put his hands up and said go ahead.

I got on my knees in the aisle and placed one hand on her chest and one on her back. I closed my eyes and asked for a miracle.

I reached for her with my awareness, I called her with my presence, and demanded for her to come back to her body. She began to move slightly, and vomited, still not conscious. None of this seemed unusual, disgusting, or unnatural.

I could perceive the worry and concern at this, and I reached for her, telling her that everyone here was very concerned and she needed to get back to her body, open her eyes and let everyone here know she was OK. Amazingly, her eyes fluttered and slowly opened.

With one hand on her back and the other using the paper towels the flight attendants handed me to clean up the front of her I just stayed there totally present with her.

She gazed at me with watery deep brown eyes and said how

good her back felt where I was touching her. Then she said "Were you sitting at the back of the plane?"

There was a space, a silence that was tangible around us as she asked me this question. As if in the question, she was acknowledging something.

"Yes," I said. "I was. Someone loves you very much and they asked me to come be with you right now, is that OK?"

"Yes," she said.

There was something different in her eyes, there was a presence and a knowing that I'd never seen before. She was then able to get up and change her messy shirt with the flight attendant and I walked back to my seat and sat back down, as if nothing ever happened.

The wonderful woman who encouraged me to get up and follow my awareness asked me what happened. I sat there spacey and wondered that myself. I was almost unbelieving of what had just so easily and naturally unfolded.

Towards the end of the flight I walked up to the front to use the bathroom. On my way back to my seat a man reached out and took my arm. He looked at me directly in the eyes and thanked me for my courage to get up, and for what I had done. It was not his words that touched me but the energy and presence in his eyes very much like the woman who had just regained consciousness.

Again, at baggage claim, another passenger approached me to thank me. Again, there was that light, that presence, something undefinable shining at me that I could not deny was there. My heart swelled at noticing this, and I was filled with a deep acknowledgment and gratitude like I had not experienced before.

As I left the airport and headed into San Francisco, the light was glimmering in everything and everyone; in the sunlight that reflected off of the leaves on the trees, in the eyes of the homeless people, in everything around me there was the same energy, the life, the consciousness, it was everywhere in everything and I could not deny my awareness of it, its existence or that I was part of it.

It was only recently that I began to ask the question, "What was the miracle here?"

For many, the miracle would seem to be the woman waking up and being totally fine and healthy. But when I asked this question, it was not this that was a miracle. It was the moment I chose. The moment I chose to rally all of my courage and step up and be me with no conclusion, no judgment, no limitations but as the question of, "What is possible here?" The miracle was for me to drop my fixed points of view about who I was and who I was not. It was for me to open up and to allow my awareness to expand, to include all of life and be the energy, the space, and consciousness that I am and that is available in every moment, in everything.

And in those hours that followed, as I allowed myself to be with this new awareness, I knew I was not alone, and for all those years of feeling so separate and alone that this amazing consciousness had been there all along. I could perceive consciousness in everything, and perceive that this consciousness was aware of me, and so very grateful for my existence, and willingness to interact and embrace possibility. Attempting to fit in and belong in this reality all those years had required me to cut off my natural awareness of the consciousness in everything.

So you see, the miracle was becoming aware. Aware of the consciousness that permeates everything and that is part of everyone. The miracle was choosing to be more me than I had ever known was possible. The miracle was being the space, energy and consciousness of no judgment, no conclusion, and of wonder, and possibility. Everything was included, nothing was separate, and nothing was judged. I was suddenly aware of a presence, an awareness that included every part of life. Acknowledging and being acknowledged, honoring and being honored by consciousness, everything all at once.

In that moment, when I chose to be all of me, to stand up and move forward no matter what awaited me, I allowed my awareness to expand to include everything. I was not more than I was before, I just dropped the points of view about who I was, who I was not, and what was possible. What if the only thing that keeps you disconnected from all of the awareness and expansiveness of you are points of view that likely are not even yours?

I share this story, and I am curious if you will find yourself within it. There is an energy I invite you to be aware of that maybe you have been aware of all of your life. My desire is that you will perceive the presence of all of life that is shining at you from everywhere and everything, caring for you, honoring all that you are, not judging you, embracing all of you and acknowledging the gift that you are.

What if what occurred on that flight with this beautiful woman for me was something that is so very natural for us? And when I say us, I mean you. I don't share this story with you to brag or make myself something greater than you. For you have capacities and you are something that goes far beyond anything you can imagine right now, do you know that?

You see, for me the energy of expansion is where you include all of you as an infinite being. It is where you understand you are not separate from anything in the universe. May you see that the universe is not something outside of you that is higher or greater than you. What if you are it? What if the ease, beauty, and consciousness you seek is actually already you? Are you willing to be the great and expansive you that includes everything when you stop judging or excluding any part of you?

I invite you to take another moment here. Just notice the space around you and the sense with your body. Are you any lighter? Is there any more space you are willing to occupy than when you started reading this chapter?

I invite you to consider that you are living and being the energy of expansion as you open up to new possibilities and acknowledge the greatness of you and what you know is possible.

What if now is the time for being as different and as great as you are, no longer trying to fit in? What if with the consciousness and energy that is in everything all around, you can choose to create a different future; a world of kindness, thriving, magic, possibilities, communion and caring for our planet. Are you ready to be in a world you know is possible and have always known is possible. What if now is the time? Will you be the miracle you know you are? And I invite you into the awareness that includes all of life, and judges nothing, and this will change our world.

Thank you for being you and for your courage to choose and be the different you be. I know I'm choosing and I'm so grateful to be on this great adventure with you.

ABOUT THE AUTHOR: MELANIE CLAMPIT

Melanie Clampit is an Access Consciousness® Certified Facilitator & Right Voice for You™ Breakthrough facilitator with 12 years of in-depth study in transformation and empowerment.

Melanie is a walking testimonial of our incredible capacity to change and transform using the Access Consciousness® tools coupled with a relentless desire for more and never giving up. After overcoming years of depression and insecurity and creating a happy, thriving living she

is now dedicated to sharing the very tools and awareness that assisted her in changing what she once believed unchangeable.

Melanie empowers you to know that you know, to trust and follow what is true for you, to create the life and world you truly desire through simple pragmatic tools that invite and inspire change and transformation from awareness, allowance, kindness, and no-judgment.

She is committed to creating a world of consciousness and awareness where we can be present with all of life, judge nothing and have the joy of living, prosperity, a healthy life and planet that will sustain a thriving future for us all.

When Melanie is not facilitating classes or seeing clients she delights in her beautiful companion, Phoenix Rising, a magical mythical horse who occasionally co-facilitates classes. Pleasures of living include traveling the world, being in nature, beauty, horseback riding, music, dancing, and experiencing new adventures. And most recently co-authoring books that facilitate a happier, more consciousness and aware world.

Chapter 5

The Space of Being That Creates Infinite Choice

By Heather Smith

W e are all familiar with the energies of contraction. When it seems like the best or only choice is to make ourselves less than, shrink away, hide, judge ourselves as wrong, bad or somehow damaged or stupid. When we don't fit and don't get what other people seem to get; times when we feel like we can't be ourselves. How often does it appear that limitation, judgment, wrongness and being small looks like the best way to manage a person or situation?

Can I ask you, does it truly work to create the result you were looking for? Kind of, sort of, maybe, temporarily?

What if there is a totally different possibility just as readily available to you in every situation, no matter what you are faced with? There is always a different possibility; in and as the energies of expansion. Where nothing is judged and the space you are can never be diminished or shrunken by anyone or anything, save your own choice to do so.

Would you be willing to be that different? Would you be willing to travel a different path, one that includes and allows you being? The choice is yours and the choice is always available to you.

The following will be several examples and possible choices to contribute to you knowing the energies of expansion and the space of being possible for you.

What does it take to get to the energies of expansion?

Acknowledge when you have had it before:

Have you ever noticed how when your relationship ends, a job ends or you lose someone in your life; at first you think how horrible it is and then some time later you look back and realize it was one of the greatest things that ever happened because of everything else that showed up in your life after that? That is the energy of expansion.

Expansion never looks how you think it will.

What if your life already has an energy of expansion you have not yet recognized?

What else can you choose that would increase the possibilities for expansion even more? What if every day of your life has the possibility for the energies of expansion to increase? What if you can create it? What if you can choose it? What if you can receive it?

What would it take to allow the energies of expansion to increase in your life, no matter what it looks like and no matter what it takes?

What are some things you can choose to increase the energies of expansion in your life?

Nature is Expansive

Do you ever notice how when you are out in nature it is so easy to relax, let down all the barriers, let go of the incessant judgment and wrongness of you and simply be? Have you noticed how there is an effortless space of expansion available when you are in nature?

One of the things that I liked to do when I was a kid was stand on the edge of a ridge top that had a rock outcropping. The long meandering meadows would stretch out below the rock outcropping for almost a mile. During the summertime after the heat of the day, the wind would blow up the long meadow. As the air moved across the tall dry golden grass it would make ripples and looked just like the ocean.

On the edge of the rocks, you could take a step back and there would be no wind at all. Take one step forward and winds would blow across your body.

I would stand in the warm wind as it caught hold of my long hair. The softness of the air caressed my cheeks and embraced my body. I would reach out with all of my senses expanding the space I was being so that it was as if the wind itself blew right through me. The very cells of my body would begin to hum and buzz. Everything about being alive felt wonderful. My body's sensory pleasure of feeling the elements of the earth combined with the simple joy of being there at that moment as all of me. It was at moments like this that I embodied the energies of expansion and the space of being.

What areas of your life do you allow that kind of presence and ease of being you? Is it only in nature? Only when you are by yourself? What would it take to increase the expansive space of being no matter where you are, no matter what you are doing, no matter who is around?

If you have been in nature and ever had this kind of sense of spaciousness and expansion, then you are capable of having it while in the city, while faced with angry and judgmental people, while in rush hour traffic, when your child or spouse is upset. All those energies are still available to you. You can ask for them and choose to be them even in those moments.

For me those moments on the ridge top embody the energy of expansion. Where everything is possible. Where nothing is judged or a wrongness. Where everything about the being I truly am is embraced, invited and welcome. It is something I choose...What if you have that choice too? What will it take for you to get there? Choosing it. Asking for it. Practicing reaching for it.

Is there a place in nature, or an activity that gives you that sense of the joy of being you, having a body and being present with everything...like you and everything is okay? What would it take for you to add more of that to your everyday life?

Add to your life the things that invite and nurture that for you. It might be nature. It might be movement of your body like a sport or dance. Or it might be creative like writing, painting or acting. Whatever it is that gives you that sense of the joy of being you and the joy of being alive - that is the energy of expansion you have available right now. Again, you can ask for it, you can choose it, you can be it.

No barriers

Intensity and density, upset and anger, depression and morose can appear to be more real because they are so heavy, loud and demanding. Whereas space is well, spacey, light, a feather touch. Does it make it any less real? The air is never less present, less available, yet it is so spacious we usually don't notice it. What if the choices and ability to expand and be space are like the air? Always present and available to choose, right now.

A very quick way to get to those energies of expansion is to lower your barriers. It is not a question of "how," it is that you can. Ask it of yourself, demand it of yourself and you will begin. You can sense it. You know when you have your barriers up. With your barriers up, you contract, you want to fight and be right. This creates separation as though getting away will protect you.

What will really protect you, as well as give you the ability to change any situation, is to expand, lower all of your barriers and expand.

It may seem impossible in the moment. It may seem like you are for sure going to die if you let down your barriers. Try it. You will find that you do not drop dead. It might even totally transform both you and the situation you are in, or the interaction you are having with another person.

Here is an example from my own life. One time my dad came home angry. This was not an unusual event. I never knew exactly what it was creating the anger, he just had a way of sharing it with everyone on a daily basis. For many years when he was "in a mood" my brothers and I would be walking on egg shells. We would do anything and everything we could to shrink ourselves and contract into something that hopefully would not invoke more anger and upset. Boy was my dad good at manipulation and control. He always got a reaction.

One day I was in a good mood. I was relaxed and happy to be

me. Dad came in with his usual upset and I had no barriers to it whatsoever. No reaction, no alteration or shrinking of me. No point of view about it. I didn't make it real or buy into it. He was not wrong for it. I remember thinking to myself; "Okay, dad is being grumpy pants, that's nice. I wonder how long he will keep it up?" To my surprise it only lasted about five minutes. What normally could go on for hours lasted only minutes! Wow, now that I was not expecting. Neither was he. Later that evening he actually commented about it. He thanked me for not reacting to him like I usually did with my own upset, withdrawal and contraction.

It was in that moment when he acknowledged, and he noticed it too, that I realized EVERYTHING is a choice and a creation. Our moods, our upset, to buy into it or not. How we handle everything is a choice and we have unlimited number of choices available in every moment. I recognized that it was a moment-by-moment choice for me that day. I could go down the usual road of putting up my barriers, or not. I also noticed it was actually easier to keep my barriers down.

Exercising that choice to lower our barriers is a powerful practice that allows us to embody the energies of expansion no matter what we are faced with.

Are you going to let "uncomfortable" stop you?

Sometimes the energy of expansion is uncomfortable. Especially when we are going beyond what we are used to. When we are going into something unknown and that we think is not possible. When we are choosing something we have not chosen before, or in a long time.

An example of that for me was actually about getting out of debt. I came to realize I was more comfortable with the energies of struggle, lack and the difficulty of having little to no money...what was really uncomfortable was the very idea of being totally present with my financial situation. I was doing anything and everything I could to avoid having honesty and clarity with myself about money. All the energies it brought up I would do anything to avoid; until the day came that I had enough.

I did not care how uncomfortable it was, I did not care what I had to face, what I had to do, what I had to look at or what I might find out about myself. I was going to step into all that uncomfortable and be with it until I was no longer uncomfortable.

Get this. Having no money was comfortable for me. Having too much money, ease with money and being present with money was totally uncomfortable. I had to be willing to be uncomfortable to change how I was functioning. By being willing to be uncomfortable it changed everything. I was beginning to be all the things and energies that I was before refusing.

I not only demanded of myself that I step into and towards all the energies of uncomfortable with money, I also demanded of myself that I expand the space I was being with money.

Before making this demand of myself, when it came to everything about bills and money I would contract myself, shrink away, make myself smaller and less present as if that would stop it. That never worked. So I started to make different choices. I started to go into the uncomfortable and also to expand when I looked at a bill or anything to do with money. Expanding the space I was being allowed things to begin changing with more ease.

When you are being space, then no matter what intensity, judgment, ugliness, contraction, anger or upset gets thrown at you or that you have about yourself; it passes right through you. It becomes just an energy and there is no energy that can harm you or make you less, unless you choose to let it.

All energies can actually contribute to you if you allow it. When you allow it, that experience is choosing to function from the energy of expansion. Expansion is when you have so much allowance for everything and everyone that shows up, that all of it becomes a contribution to you having more of you. The doors of possibility open and everything you ask for can actualize in your life in magical and unexpected ways.

No judgment

There is no such thing as negative energy except that people's judgments make it that way for them. It does not have to be that way for you, however. Without the judgment of bad or good, right or wrong; you are able to be aware of all energies and what is coming your way. Without judgment of how an energy feels, you can choose to change the energies. Or, if you can't change it you will know when not to be there the stuff you would really not like to experience. You can avoid dangerous and unpleasant situations when you have no judgment of the energies you are aware of.

For example, if you have no judgment of a rapist, you will know when someone is willing to do that and you can choose accordingly. You can get away from the person and situation that would create you at the effect of the rapist, instead of being a victim to it because you don't wish to know the person in front of you is capable of such a thing.

It is not wrong to be aware of the ugly things people choose to be and do. It does not mean you are judgmental if you are aware of the negative. It means you have choice.

As the energy of expansion, you would include awareness of everything; the good, the bad and the ugly. You no longer have to be at the effect of other people and their meanness, cruelty, control, smallness or limitation. You never have to limit you again.

It is an incredibly powerful and empowering choice to be the energy of expansion in the face of everything that shows up in your life. It is your choice to have it, create it and be it.

The choice to expand and be the space of you is always available.

What would it be like to allow yourself to play with all this? Explore, practice, who knows, maybe even enjoy yourself in the process of discovering just how powerful and capable you really are.

Now my friend, what will you choose?

ABOUT THE AUTHOR: HEATHER P. SMITH

 Heather P. Smith has worked with a variety of different energy modalities for over twenty-one years. Using the transformation of energies in her body and life to heal herself of Asthma; she knows from her own life experience the power of choice and question to transform what most people consider unchangeable.

Heather says "by developing our capacities for being aware of energy and utilizing our natural ability to change the energies we are functioning as, there is no limit to what can be healed and created as our body and our life.

It is our choices we make moment by moment, day by day that create and contribute to everything that is showing up as our life right now. Change your choices and you change how your entire life shows up. This is the potency you have available to you already. Have you been using your capacity for choice for you or against you?"

An Access Consciousness® Facilitator for over nine year, Heather has found Access to be the easiest modality for changing any area of life.

The straight-forward simplicity of Access should not be underestimated in its potency and power for transforming energy and providing clarity to those who play with it.

Heather has always been a pragmatist. If she can't use a modality easily in her everyday life and get true and lasting change from its use; she is not interested. Nothing has been more easy to use and simply to apply than the tools of awareness from Access Consciousness®. Empowering people to know that they know is the tag line of Access, and it complements what Heather strives for in facilitation; for a client to know they are the creator of their own life and they have the ability to change anything if they are willing to go on the adventure of discovering what it will take.

www.heathersmith.accessconsciousness.com
www.endingptsd.com
www.heatherpsmith.com

Chapter 6

The Expansion of Your Golden Heart

By Sylvie Olivier

After 45 years of experiencing a life of duality where I struggled on all fronts, a brand new possibility presented itself to me. Old patterns, belief systems and memories transmitted from my family, generation after generation were released once I allowed myself to dive very deeply into my own Essence. This new way of being opened me up to a state of fluidity where I once again found myself being one with my Essence, where the mind no longer interfered with opportunities coming my way.

I now receive inspirations, intuitions, ideas and resources with vivid clarity and answers manifest themselves through the profound knowledge of the highest potential for my life. My life is now filled with magnificent opportunities that make my heart sing every single day. I don't have to work for them to show up in my life, I simply allow these opportunities, resources, clients, partners, friends and even money to find me. How cool is that!?

The most exciting part of it all is that YOU can live your life that way too! This is what I call Golden Heart Living! Our Golden Heart is this sacred space inside our hearts and it is the most direct doorway to our Essence. It's a very powerful tool for expansion, which we will discuss later.

I asked myself, what if?

What if it's possible to live in a state of complete Neutrality? What if it's possible to let Creation manifest itself through you instead of trying to create the life of your dreams? Would you like that? Would you be open and willing to experience this state of Neutrality?

Allow me to explain what I mean by Neutrality before saying your big vibrational YES! And keep in mind that simply reading the words on this page will begin the process of releasing crystallized emotions. You don't have to do anything other than stay open and be willing to experience something completely different.

Every word of this chapter has been encoded with Pure Love and with the Gold Consciousness of the Golden Heart of All That Is, so you don't even have to do anything for it to work! As you read the words, activations will occur and you'll open yourself up to expansion in a way words can't describe!

The Duality of Vibrational Frequencies

Before I go any further with the Expansion of Your Golden Heart, I'd like to invite you to stop for a minute and take a look at a few energetic aspects of human life: thoughts, emotions and beliefs.

For nearly two decades, I studied different forms of energy. I wanted to understand what had happened to my daughter while she was so terribly sick. She went from having about 6 to 7 hours to live to being completely healed, whole and complete. My daughter's illness had been such a shock that finding a cure became a personal quest, which in turn transmuted into a new way of living, the way of Golden Heart Living.

Sharing information

The following is a visual description which I received, to share and explain the process experienced by human beings when they're first separated from their Essence and then go back to being one with it.

During the third trimester of pregnancy, we had to prepare ourselves to come into this world. While still in our mother's womb, we enveloped ourselves with a thin layer of lead (figuratively speaking of course). We needed to make sure that we would survive once we arrived in the physical world; we thought we had to adapt and alter our true Essence in order to be loved and taken care of. That's when the ego/personality started to form. That's also when we started separating ourselves from our Essence.

When we came into this world as a newborn, and during the first seven years of our life, our brain used theta waves. We were like sponges and we absorbed everything around us. That's when our family and cultural environments programmed us with a set of beliefs, thoughts and emotions that we now bathe in. It's neither good nor bad, it simply is what it is! As the years passed, the layer of lead thickened until we found ourselves wearing a complete form fitting armor that went from our head down to our toes (again, figuratively speaking).

As young children, we convinced ourselves that we needed this lead armor to protect ourselves from the outside world. As we moved into our teenage years, we tried our best to get noticed, acknowledged and loved; albeit, probably not always the way our parents would have liked! We grew up with the duality of right and wrong; and of course, we desperately wanted to be right! We longed to be the best so that our tribe would accept us and therefore, we'd be proud of ourselves. We also wanted to belong, achieve success and live our dreams OUR OWN WAY.

We carried on with our way of being into adulthood where our armor reached gladiator status; very thick, solid and completely polarized, acting as a magnet. In this state of consciousness, our lives are dictated by the daily grind and we delude ourselves into thinking that we're free to choose our lifestyle. We're not aware that we're prisoners to our own thoughts, beliefs and emotions. And then... for some people, something dramatic happens in their life: the death of a loved one, a health crisis, different kinds of abuse, divorce or maybe even bankruptcy. For others, a simple awakening begins to emerge. The result is the same for everyone; we all start to feel trapped in our armor since we know deep down that there's more to life than what we've chosen to settle for. Regardless of what triggered the awakening, we all then feel the urgency to find a new way of living and of course, life presents us with an opportunity to return to our Essence.

And so begins our own quest to find answers with what's available around us. We experience a plethora of personal development techniques, each one confirming the fact that the armor that we're trapped in has started to be very uncomfortable. We therefore courageously chose to move forward, despite the fear. And when the first piece of our armor cracks open... oh my, isn't that destabilizing!!! It's like falling into an abyss without a single point of reference or anything to hold on to.

So many wonderful people are in this phase right now, facing their beliefs and feeling the crystallized emotions in their body... So, if that's what you're experiencing right now, know that you're not alone. The Universe is there for you and in this very moment, you're surrounded by Pure Love! And the Universe is using me as an instrument to deliver this message to YOU!

Breathe in... Breathe out...

Breathe in... Breathe out...

Breathe in... Breathe out...

The quickest way to dissolve your armor is by breathing! Our breath is like a beautiful wave that dissolves thought patterns, belief systems and crystallized emotions that were created in duality consciousness. This natural and simple process of breathing will clear the way for you to receive inspirations, resources and ideas with clarity. And it'll allow you to feel the Love that you're made of. Big pieces of the armor will fall off, offering you more freedom and more space to shine your light! This stage represents the chaos that often precedes expansion. So breathe into the chaos! Free yourself!

Once the armor surrounding us has dissolved, we're still covered by a lead structure, but a much lighter one. It's very similar to the thin layer of lead that covered us in the womb. We become more conscious and aware of thoughts, beliefs and emotions. We're still controlled by the magnetic grid but we start realizing that we're not this structure. We are neither our thoughts nor our beliefs and we are not the crystallized emotions in our body. We're so much more!!! We feel free and liberated once we know that we're not this structure and we become aware that all thoughts, emotions, beliefs, opinions and judgments rooted in this structure don't mean anything about who we are!

Accessing fluidity through Neutrality

When we begin to access Neutrality, the lead structure still surrounds our Essence, but we feel with our heart and we hear and listen to the inner voice that whispers messages of Pure Love. The veil blinding our view becomes thinner and thinner. Once we get that we're not just our thoughts, beliefs and emotions, the structure that previously enveloped us no longer surrounds our body. We can now see the structure, almost like a physical form, right in front of us. When we allow this structure of lead consciousness to peel off of our body, we can then fully receive our Essence, comprised of Golden Light. By doing so, we fill every part of our body with Gold Consciousness, with Pure Love. This kind of Love is the fabric that we're made of and its purpose is to expand into every possible shape and form of Pure Love. Our Golden Heart is completely filled with Pure Love as we send out a ray of the purest Love straight into the old structure that consisted of all the old emotions, thought patterns and belief systems.

As the vibrational frequency rises, the old lead structure starts to vibrate more and more intensely, allowing the lead structure to transform into minuscule lead particles that vibrate so intensely that they simply detach from the old structure. The vibration continues to rise to allow transmutation to occur. What was ingrained in the lead structure has now been transmuted into gold particles, and then into Pure Golden Light emanating into the entire Universe. We then break free from the magnetic grid and transcend the Law of Attraction. We are Pure Creator Consciousness having a physical experience in a body, on a planet. That's simply beautiful!!! We're no longer polarized. We live in blissful Neutrality, completely free of duality/polarity, no longer impacted by the outside world!

Welcome to the Expansion of Your Golden Heart

Your Golden Heart is a sacred space where you can gravitate from a reality that includes 'trying hard'; achieving goals with great effort and a focus on personal development. Instead, by connecting with your Divine Essence, the life of your dreams flows naturally and easily to you. You team up with the Universe and become a co-creator to welcome love, abundance, optimal health and everything and anything that's already available and waiting for you. You live in the fluidity of Neutrality!

Through this level of Expansion, the Universe provides you with all the resources you need for fluid neutrality. You'll know what it feels like to be loved, cherished, honored, nurtured and taken care of with the best of the best, with no shortcuts at all. You are Pure Creator Consciousness and you manifest with grace and ease. You allow yourself to be taken care of and welcome the abundance of gifts that the Universe has in store for you. You receive and welcome Pure Love and you're one with your Essence! You awaken to the most magical part of you!

To assist you in moving toward the Expansion of your own Golden Heart, I'll share nine very profound principles that you can play with on a daily basis. It's when I first began the expansion of my Golden Heart that I received these high vibrational tools that have become the principles that allowed me to experience many cycles of Expansion since then. Each principle vibrates at a very high frequency and by regularly playing with them; you'll start to feel them as they unfold in your consciousness.

Ready...Let's dance!

The 9 Principles of Golden Heart Wisdom

Are you open to letting yourself express mastery?

This is when you let everything come to you with grace and ease. You allow yourself to receive, as you're one with your Essence. You're like a butterfly that was once a caterpillar and expanded into this gorgeous and vibrant instrument of Divinity. You now fluidly dance with every opportunity that life brings to you! You're free to move and experience the full potential of your life.

As you allow transmutation to occur, you move from lead

consciousness created through thought patterns, belief systems and crystallized emotions; towards Gold Consciousness, where you express your Essence throughout your life with fluid grace.

In your Golden Heart, you're whole and complete... you're perfect as you are. You don't need to be fixed because you're not broken. You don't need to become a better person, or learn something new before you get there. You are perfect as you are, here and now.

Are you willing to co-create an extraordinary life?

This is when you know your Self as whole and complete. You stop trying so hard to become a better person and improve yourself. You stop your personal quest of always wanting to learn more and you acknowledge your Essence in its divine beauty. You allow the magnificent perfection that you are to be unveiled as you connect to your Golden Heart, the most direct doorway to your Essence.

As your own vibrational frequency rises, you know you're whole and complete. The beauty of this experience is that you'll have the profound knowledge that this is the Truth!

In your Golden Heart, you're connected to the Source of All That Is... Abundance is no longer a concept that you long for... you are Abundance in all its forms therefore Abundance fills your life in every sphere. You have an Abundance of love, creativity, joy, fun and wonder; excitement and adventure... an Abundance of wealth... also in the form of money...money is your great friend!

Are you willing to tune in to the Source of All That Is?

This is when you allow Abundance to come into your life without working for it or wanting to create something in your life. You have this deep knowledge that YOU are Abundance in all its forms, and you let it fill every aspect of your life! By unlocking your highest potential, you access all the riches the Universe has in store for you.

As you welcome infinite Abundance into your life, you're filled with profound joy! You're open to receiving inspirations, ideas, intuitions and a multitude of resources that'll allow you to create the life of your dreams with grace and ease via the clear conduit that you are.

In your Golden Heart, you see perfection in everything... even within your own imperfections and the imperfections of those around you. Guilt and shame are no longer partners in your life... you are completely FREE... free of judgment, of opinions and of beliefs of any kind. You're connected to the Real You... you know you're an Infinite Being with infinite choices and possibilities.

Are you willing to see perfection in everything?

This is when you're at peace with what you perceive as imperfections. You're free of the patterns and agreements that maintained you in duality. You feel the freedom of being connected to the real YOU and infinite choices and possibilities present themselves. What's truly amazing is that you can clearly see through your own eyes that you've let go of your judgments and perceptions!

As you free yourself from the outside world and let it be as is, you become ONE with the Universe and you embrace the neutrality of the heart. You're peaceful, joyful and loving! You allow yourself to live beautiful, fantastic, amazing experiences! You live every day with profound joy - no matter what comes up! You walk into the world, free of any impact it has on you.

In your Golden Heart, you express your Divine Essence in

every moment of your life. You embody your Divine Essence in your physical body that vibrates at a very high frequency. Your cells receive every nutrient they need in their highest form to give you optimal health.

Are you open to aligning yourself with the profound knowledge and certainty of your Divine Essence?

This is when you allow vibrant health to come to life within you! You welcome the highest frequencies to nurture your cells so that they receive every nutrient they need to express vitality. You also let Creation manifest itself through you to give birth to the expression of your highest potential.

As you reawaken to the wonder and lightness of our Divine Essence, you surf this high vibration and you come to terms with the rigidity of your reality. You allow the dissolution of patterns and beliefs that aren't who you are! You feel the sensations in your body as you let the spiral of Golden Light flow easily into each cell.

In your Golden Heart, you have access to Pure Potentialities... you have NO limits! You're limitless and infinite... you no longer need to understand and figure things out with your cognitive mind in a contracted way. You have this deep knowing inside you... inside this tiny sacred space of your Golden Heart, which is the heart of the Heart where you access the Mind of God.

Are you open to accessing the Pure Potentialities of the Universe?

This is when you are limitless and infinite while basking in a field of infinite possibilities. You let your work, your life, your dreams and your body play together to create the most fabulous symphony as you watch your full Divine potential awaken! You remember what it feels like to have fun just for the sake of it. The special energy of Christmas is felt every day as you let awesome and amazing potentialities manifest in your life.

As you allow this deep knowledge to grow within, you tap into the energy of what makes your heart sing. You're open to creating a fabulous dance as you express your uniqueness, your wholeness and your pristine completeness!

In your Golden Heart, you express your fundamental nature. You're fully present. You're no longer attached to heavy emotions, you no longer resist. You're completely open and free to allow fun, wonder, joy, enthusiasm, freedom, love, adventure, excitement and exuberance to flow through the Infinite Being that you are.

Are you willing to let your fundamental nature express itself through you?

This is when you know yourself as the Master of Love that you are. You let yourself experience what it feels like to totally and completely be one with your Essence. You exponentially receive as you choose to stop holding on to memories and limitations. While you come to terms with heavy emotions, memories and patterns, you'll feel the same kind of freedom as does a bird flying from its nest, sharing its beauty and light everywhere it goes.

As you allow your light to shine into the world with grace and fluidity, you'll experience lightness of the heart, lightness of the spirit and lightness in your life! You'll feel the purest joy of being one with your Essence!

In your Golden Heart, miracles and magic are no longer a fairy-tale. The reality that you know as real realigns itself to match your high vibration, so what may seem miraculous and magical become part of your daily life.

Are you willing to watch how magic and miracles are no longer a fairy-tale in your own life?

This is when you enjoy the magic of being loved, nurtured, cherished and honored as the walking, talking miracle that you are. You already know how to do this! This is YOU!!! By allowing the Universe to take care of you, you'll see your reality realign itself to match your high vibration! Therefore, what may seem miraculous and magical to others will be part of your daily life!

As you give full command to your Golden Heart, you'll watch the real magic of life unfold into your own experience! You'll discover the magic of living a luxurious life while being very intimate with your Divine Essence!

In your Golden Heart, you easily access the silence between thoughts. This space is where the tiny particles of consciousness come together to bring the life of your dreams into reality. Reality with a capital R, the Reality of Divine Consciousness...your Infinite Reality!

Are you open to accessing the Master Alchemist within?

This is when you tap into the highest levels of connection with the Source. You let lead consciousness transmute itself into Gold Consciousness! You're the Master Alchemist within, creating Infinite Reality while accessing the silence between thoughts. This is where the minuscule particles of consciousness come together to bring the life of your dreams into your infinite and Divine Reality!

As you allow your Golden Heart to expand and show you the highest and best way to live your life, you'll manifest a lifestyle beyond your wildest dreams. Sacred doors will open spontaneously for you as a contribution from the Universe. You'll allow all the resources to come to life before you and you'll dance with each of them!

A word of completion

As we complete this cycle of Expansion of your Golden Heart, I invite you to play with two more divine, vibrant, pristine questions to allow YOU to expand even further!

Are you willing to recognize yourself as the magnificent and exquisite gift that you are?

Are you willing to receive Pure Love from the Universe?

My Golden Heart is wide open as I write these last words to you. I feel YOU... I know YOU... and I love YOU with the purest of LOVE!

I'd like to share with you is that YOU are loved beyond measure! There is absolutely nothing that you need to do to be worthy of this Pure Love! You are LOVED! Can you feel it? And if you don't, it doesn't matter... you're still embraced and nurtured and loved by the Universe.

I acknowledge your presence as Divine and I invite you to allow Pure Love to dissolve the lead structure that you may still be a prisoner of. I invite you with the entirety of my Golden Heart to welcome the Expansion of your Golden Heart with grace and ease!

Every word of this chapter has been encoded with Pure Love and with the Gold Consciousness of the Golden Heart of All That Is. As you read the words, activations occurred and you opened yourself up to expansion in a way that no words can accurately describe. So, I invite you to re-read it occasionally and watch the magic of your own expansion come to life, more and more! I also invite you to play with the 9 Principles of Golden Heart Wisdom! They're a very powerful tool towards your own Expansion!

I love you very deeply!

Namaste'

Sylvie

ABOUT THE AUTHOR: SYLVIE OLIVIER

Sylvie Olivier, Master Alchemist and Energy Expert, brings magic into people's lives by sharing Golden Heart Wisdom. She's on an incredibly inspiring journey: to assist humanity in expressing their true Divine Essence. If you've ever had the opportunity of meeting Sylvie, you'd agree that her bountiful energy and huge heart transpires through all of her interactions. She gives you towards the realization that when you're aligned with your true Essence, your vibrational frequency increases and your heart expands to all the opportunities available to you; therefore everyone around you not only feels your high vibrational state, but they also benefit from its uplifting influence.

After 45 years of living a life of duality where she struggled on all fronts, Sylvie suddenly saw that a new possibility was available. Rather than living a life fueled by duality, she realized that neutrality offered a direct passageway to our Essence. That's when she became a yes and dove right in to her own Essence. This new state of being opened her up to a state of fluidity where she was once again one with her Essence. Her mind no longer interfered with opportunities that came her way.

Today, in her state of expansion, she receives inspirations, intuitions, ideas and resources with vivid clarity and answers manifest themselves through the profound knowledge of the highest potential for her life. Her life is now filled with magnificent opportunities that make her heart sing every single day. She's given up on working hard to achieve things and rather, she simply allows these opportunities, resources, clients, partners, friends and even money to find her. Pretty amazing, right!?

Today, Sylvie assists people in connecting with their true Essence, their own unique gifts and purpose to truly express their authentic divine selves. Once they are able to connect with their pure Essence, they are then ready for major shifts in expansion.

Through her signature process, Sylvie activates people's Golden Hearts; the most direct doorway to their Divine Essence and is a sacred space inside each of us, where everything is possible. This space of high energetic vibrational frequency transmutes ancient beliefs and patterns, fears, heaviness and emotions (what she calls Lead Consciousness) into profound joy and the free expression of our Highest Self, our divine Essence (what she calls Gold Consciousness).

In Gold Consciousness, our heart opens to the divinity of our Essence. Our body aligns with its innate intelligence. In this state of consciousness, we do not have to do anything, we're simply who we are and are ready and open to dance with the opportunities that the universe presents us. It's phenomenal how a few inspired actions produce extraordinary results when we welcome our intuitions, opportunities, resources and ideas, rather than searching for them.

In addition to Sylvie's expansive life experiences of connecting with her own Divine Essence and living the life she was meant for, she also studied

Bioenergetics for more than 7 years at the Alternative Medicine College of Canada. For over ten years, Sylvie was a well-known health adviser and teacher as she continued to learn a multitude of modalities such as quantum physics and sacred geometry, always wanting to enrich her practice. She's also a certified practitioner of the Emotional Freedom Technique (EFT) as well as of The One Command Method and the Getting Thru Techniques (GTT) that she studied at the Awakenings Institute. She is also a Certified Dream Coach®, from the Dream University®. She now integrates her training as a musician and the use of high energetic vibrational frequency essential oils into her practice.

Sylvie offers different group and individual programs, online and offline. To learn more about her work and to tap into your highest frequencies, visit her website: www.goldenheartwisdom.com.

Chapter 7

The Valley of Life: The Key to Expansion

"Open the Door...I'm Waiting to Come In!"

By Maria Dempsey, CMM

"Every Flower is a Soul... blossoming in nature." ~ Gerard De Nerval

Have you ever been in a valley in your life and didn't know how you got there? Why is this happening to me? I thought I was bright, sharp, on top of the world, unstoppable, the best in my field, always creating new ideas for my business/company, showing my value, the "go to person", in the know and flow, practicing personal growth, gratitude, and love. How did this all change for me? Why me and why now?

It's always challenging to change or have something taken away and pulled from under us. Here are the more common losses we experience: losing someone we love, a job, a house, a promotion, a family member, close friend, boyfriend, girl-friend, our health, or money. How do we explain this loss or change in our life and sudden shift of energy? How do we adjust from here?

"How long do we stay in the valley?" How does it feel to be small, fearful, helpless, worried, frustrated, failure, need to be right, blame, and guilt, denial, jealous or resentful? How do we get out?

We have all been here, some longer than others. What do we do when this happens to us? How do we pick up off the ground and keep going? I heard the statement, "if we can look up, we can get up."

The big question we must ask ourselves is: How have we attracted this circumstance into our life? There are no acci-dents. Things happen for a reason and that reason is to serve us, a lesson to be learned, and a transition that needs to take place in our life. It's all about how we move forward versus go backward.

By accepting and receiving our own goodness, we take the first step toward expansion and prosperity. Once we appre-ciate what we have, want to expand, and believe we deserve more, we will expand.

Are we accepting to expand, be open and receptive to receive, or are we blocking it from coming in? One of the most difficult steps we take is allowing to receive the good that we are due. We are too conditioned to worry, struggle, find excuses, or stay in the fear. We could make excuses all the time of why we can't have it or deserve it. Have you ever asked yourself these expanding questions, "What can we do to get that, do that, become that? What is possible?" We give up three feet before we found the diamond. We end up missing the diamond because of our mindset.

I have been in the valley before. This happened to me several times. In one instance, I had an international business that was thriving. I visited Singapore for business a few times a year. On one of my visits coming home from Singapore, I got a call saying we were pulling out of our business and moving to another business. I was reluctant to move as I was making the money I aspired and was in the flow of good business and growth, didn't want to give up what I had built and start all over. I gave up a $20,000 a month income to start all over. It was devastating and took me awhile to get over.

The next business I went to never got off the ground like the first, the company went bankrupt. I put a lot of money and time into it. The company's stock went down to a penny stock and then went bankrupt. I lost all my stock, left the business to find something more stable, and could never look back. I still had regrets of giving up my international business and how I could have grown their international markets. I had to forgive and move on. It wasn't easy; it was a transformation in progress. I had to be willing to have faith that something better would open its doors.

Instead of taking it personally, look at what's not going right or getting upset about the situation, I went on a Personal Development journey. As part of this journey, I read over 30 books, attended over 20 workshops, spent over $20,000 in one year on personal development, and worked on me.

There was a part of my transformation and a period in my life that I had the honor to work with John Assaraf from the movie "The Secret" and Bonnie Bruderer, who worked for Tony Robbins for many years. I worked as an independent representative for them and was trained to do Vision Boards and Vision training to help corporations, non-profits, boards of directors, special interest groups, and customers from many walks of life. This Visioning process was a step toward helping them move closer to their goals with plan, action steps and deliverables.

As part of my transformation, I felt a calling to become a coach, and was a very successful one. I had customers who requested me to return to help another department, special interest groups, non-profit organizations, boards of directors, spiritual centers, yoga centers, Café Gratitude events, and more. It was a massive growth expansion in my life. I continue to do Vision Board Training and the Visioning process and schedule events for new and existing clients and may be willing to do this for you. I am very select with the clients I choose to do these events due to the nature of the work.

I am a "Visionary" and enjoy planting seeds, mapping out a vision with their goals, supporting the process and watching it take flight. We use very powerful, life changing, and transformational tools. In the process, I am grateful of the inspiration, growth and expansion in my life and the ability to reinvent myself as a result of helping others.

Here are 7 Tools that I used to Expand and Reinvent Myself

1. Discover your purpose and what excites you, makes you glow, and keeps you up at night.... thinking about positively.

2. Why do I want this, what will it take? Am I passionate about it?

3. Setting specific and measurable goals

4. What is the feeling I want to have? How will it feel to have this?

5. Visualize it happening and create vivid pictures in your mind

6. Make a visual picture of the goal. Put it on a vision board

7. Be heart-centered with gratitude. Have gratitude for all that you have and all that you are accomplishing.

More About the 7 Tools to Expand and Reinvent Yourself

1. Purpose, what excites you, gives you renewed energy, makes you glow, keeps you up at night or wakes you up in the morning thinking about, strategizing? I believe our purpose comes from God. He will give us a worthwhile dream and mission. The key is if we can quiet our mind long enough to be patient, to listen for direction and allow our soul to speak within us and follow it.

2. Why do I want this? What will it take? Am I passionate about it?

What am I willing to let go of? What habits am I willing to change or give up to make room for new ones? Am I passionate about it? Does it give me joy? Am I doing this for me or to impress someone? Do I care what others think of me? Am I willing to sacrifice something or give up another habit to get what I want? What can I move out of the way that is not serving me and allow space for this new direction?

3. Specific and Measurable Goals:

SMART Goals:

Specific: Be as specific as possible. I want to lose 10 pounds by September 30th.

Measurable: Can we measure how we have achieved this goal? Number achieved etc.

Achievable: Are they achievable goals?

Realistic: Are they within reason of achieving? If our mind says that is too far away from where we are, or that they are not realistic, then consider finding a goal that we can move toward that feels better.

Timely: Can we achieve this goal within a specific date?

We need a plan to reach the goals. If we say we want to save a million dollars within one year, do we have an aggressive plan with resources, support and vehicle to accomplish this?

4. How does our goal feel to us? How does it feel in our body? It all boils down to the feeling in our body. How we feel about certain things. What is the feeling we wish to fulfill? Feel the feeling now intensely as if we have already achieved the goal. It is September 30th and I am 10 pounds lighter. How does it feel to have accomplished my goal? We want to achieve the goal, yet it is really the feeling we want to have once we receive it.

5. Visualize what is happening and create vivid pictures in your mind. What am I wearing? How smoking hot do I look? How am I strutting my sleek body etc.? Who is applauding me for my achievement? How sexy do I look and feel?

6. Put a picture of you with the outfit you plan to wear as having achieved your goal on your vision board. How does it make you feel to look at it? Look at it every day and feel the

feeling by looking at the picture and how this feels to have accomplished your goal.

7. Be heart-centered. Get in touch with the heart. Feel the connection of love for yourself and others. Develop the heart chakra and flow of love. Know that you are loved, supported, and feel the gratitude.

What's the Best Excuse You Have?

Excuses are a roadblock to our success. Whatever we tell ourselves, WE ARE RIGHT. Change the story, create new beliefs, habits, and the outcome will change.

Something I always wanted to do was get my real estate license and sell vacation ownership. I have been in the travel business almost all my life and that was one area that I did not have experience. I was interviewing at the time at several hotel companies. One flew me out for a final interview to Colorado to visit their top executives. I had three job opportunities in the hopper to be a Director of Sales and Marketing for traditional hotels. I sat down and meditated what was the next move in my career and vacation ownership came up. Guess what was on my vision board? My dream job in travel making at least $10,000 a month. I had been looking at my vision board on a daily basis for over a year, creating the feeling of what it felt like to have already achieved my goal. I finally achieved it.

I work in Member Services for one of the best vacation

ownership companies in the world. I am humbled by the compliments I receive from our customers on how I am so very different than most people in our industry. I set out to be different, to change people's lives, to help others, to transform our industry. I care more about people, their family, their future, and having quality time and vacations.

I am a vacation doctor. I hold a person accountable for what they say is important in their lives and taking vacations. One of them is spending quality time with people they love through vacationing. I was a workaholic for many years.

We bought a vacation ownership for our family and it changed the course of our vacations for life. We were forced, in a good way to take vacations. It helped grow our relationship with our daughters. We learned of interests, passions, hobbies, fears, challenges, foods we love etc. It's life changing as we spend time together, it's the beauty of life... and of the soul. Some people think, think, and think about how they can take one, can they afford one; while others just do it. By having one of our own, we got to stay in much nicer, spacious places, had the privacy for my girls, took necessary vacations, saw some of the world-domestically and international, and built quality time together. When you get right down to it, let yourself go, you deserve it!

Successful people make decisions quickly and are slow to turn back. Procrastinators make decision slowly and are quick to quit and turn back. They never get off the ground; they keep putting it off and giving reasons versus results.

When it's time to take action, guess what happens?

People make excuses for their happiness or why they can't have more of it. These reasons/excuses don't just apply just to my industry, they apply to life.

There are reasons why people deny themselves (consciously and subconsciously) and allow circumstances, mindset, or reasons that stop them.

Here are some of the reasons:

1. I'm not good enough. I don't deserve this.

2. I'm not loved, I'm not loveable, or getting much love

3. I don't have the money

4. I need to fix the ___ first, I need to do this first____

5. I work too much and can't take the time

6. I'm already good

7. I will do something about it later, tomorrow. There's never a tomorrow, it never comes. You will find another reason for not giving to yourself.

Guess what? It's a pattern and it's dictating more than one area in your life. "Today is the Day". Don't think too long as you will take yourself out of it. Just do it!

Expand Your Relationships – Expand Your Life

I am blessed with wonderful relationships in my life with family and friends. I love my girls so much. As a mother of teenage girls, I have a very joyous relationship, more so than most moms of teens. I am always so proud of them on a daily basis. I don't think of them as teenage girls, I think of them as truly ladies becoming. They are amazing, so talented, gracious, hardworking and such gems. I am grateful for my husband who has helped me through ups and downs of life. I am grateful to my dad and my stepmom for giving me an opportunity to have a different future. I am grateful to my mom also for the lessons, both good and bad that I learned.

I love my sister (one of my very best friends in life) and my two brothers. We have grown closer over the years. I am also grateful for my half-sister, my nieces and nephews, as well as my friends, Lise, Hans, Joyce, Lou, Linda and many more. These are priceless relationships. I also value my work relationships as they continue to grow and flourish.

Family and friends are priceless treasures. The more quality time spent helps put more goodness into our lives.

Who/What is holding you back? Is it you or some-one else?

Sometimes the closest people in our lives want to keep us safe. I have had people in my life discourage me from doing things that I wanted to do. Their goal was to keep me safe, in my comfort zone, fearful of change and didn't want me to take any risks. . Being safe doesn't help us grow. Our friends and family may be reluctant to change or for us to change; but change is inevitable. We can't listen to the naysayers, people trying to pull us back, the dreams stealers, the balloon poppers. We can have compassion for their concern, their feelings; however, we have to keep focused on moving forward with our goals. We don't want set-backs. Otherwise, if we don't move our life forward..., then who will achieve our goals? It begins and ends with me!

Who is in your way of achieving your greatness? Why haven't you achieved your goals yet? If you knew how to do it, you would have already done this. Are you allowing them to stop you, make you safe or keep you where you are? Why? What are you willing to do to speak up, step out and be the change you wish you see?

There is no one formula to clearing the hurdles life throws in our paths. For me, I found hard work, never giving up, determination, and a solid faith is what I needed to face the challenges that came my way. I learned that anything worth pursuing, there was always a storm before the real goal appeared. It has to get worst sometimes before it can get better. Be open, be patient and BE READY TO EXPAND!

ABOUT THE AUTHOR: MARIA DEMPSEY

Maria brings a diversified portfolio of experience including over 30 years of leadership in the travel and luxury hotel/hospitality industries, with such prestigious companies as Westin Hotels/Starwood, Pan Pacific Hotels and Resorts, and Wyndham Vacation Resorts and over 5 years in the airline industry with People Express Airlines.

She is an enlightened leader and a true entrepreneurial spirit teaching visioning, strategic planning, vision boards and overall transformational leadership with organizations, boards, corporations etc. She has grown international business, developing new business in many key countries and regions including Asia/Pacific, Caribbean, Mexico, and Canada. She was a contributing editor and helped developed the western region for the Performance Magazine, working with HNW key executives, transformational leaders, authors, speakers and business owners.

Maria has a passion for sales, marketing, leadership and serving others. Maria has multiple degrees including Aviation Management, Business Administration, with a minor in Marketing. She can be reached to conduct Vision Board Training for your group, Marketing consulting/sales and International Business via Linked In: Maria Dempsey.

Chapter 8

The Expansive Qualities of Genius

By John Hittler

You have that one person in your life—the one who holds such admirable and noticeable talent—the type that you both admire and envy. You only *wish* you could do what they do...and the ease with which they do it.

I know that person too. We all do. They seem to glide through life effortlessly. They also seem to enjoy every day, even every moment. What if that person were you? That you were secretly (or openly) admired and envied, for that specific way you are able to pull off that *one thing* with such ease! Chances are, you are that person for many people, and just never realized that when you enter a certain realm of activities, you excel like no other. You look like a "genius".

Truth is, you *are* a Genius. You are a Genius, because you

possess a genius level talent. We all do. The trick tends to be, recognizing, acknowledging, accepting, and then fully utilizing that one high level talent, in a manner that expands what is possible for you every day. Genius works that way. Exercise and engage it, and it expands. Dismiss it, and it becomes like a doorstop—useful to a point, but with limited impact on the world.

To live a truly abundant life, there are two big decisions you have to make well: your choice for life partner (spouse, significant other, close friends) and your choice of what calling you will pursue. Note, I did not suggest pursuing the correct career, instead substituting a "calling". They could be radically different, or they could be tied closely together. You can expand your universe to live the life of genius, or you can live a life attached to talent, competence, or just mere skills. The difference greatly expands and improves your life, or keeps it relegated more to the routine, mundane, and even stressful.

You can change careers. You can quit jobs. You simply cannot run away from a calling. Likewise, you cannot run away from your Genius. Here's why…

What exactly is *Genius*, and Where Does it Come From?

Consider a crime scene…one with DNA samples that have been left in the form of saliva, blood, or sweat. Now consider that the same crime scene has clearly visible fingerprints. Forensic scientists can quickly and easily identify exactly who was present at the scene, because we can prove that both the DNA and the fingerprints belong to one specific individual on the planet. Science is that precise, that our DNA and fingerprints are so unique, that no other human being in the history of mankind has ever held the same genetic blueprint as you, or as me.

Why would it then be so odd to imagine that each human being has a talent so unique, and so highly developed, that no other human being in the history of our time on earth has ever held that same talent? It makes sense, doesn't it? We already have the genetic uniqueness in the form of DNA(our unseen blueprint) and through fingerprints, our outward "signature", if you will. Why would our world class, unique talent, then, not be contained in every cell of our body? The answer quite probably points to the idea that our highest talents are embedded into every cell in our body, or our DNA!

I call that "genius" and you have one, just as unique to you, as mine is to me. Your Genius came as "factory equipment" and you 'got what you got'. I did too.

The trick is embracing what you received, so that you live your life *through* your Genius, rather than against it. Living through your Genius expands your life's possibilities, opportunities, and enjoyment. Wishing for a different Genius contracts and eliminates possibilities, opportunities, and enjoyment, and makes life much more of a struggle. One way creates abundance. The other, scarcity.

Whatever you got comes as a complete gift, and it came to you free of charge. If you're spiritual, consider it the greatest gift of talent from God. If you embrace a more scientific approach, you won the lottery—big time! Both methodologies work equally well, in describing the uniqueness, power, and beauty of genius.

So you may say, that's great, I got this talent, and I have no idea what the heck it is! Or perhaps you have a sense, but not much more than that. If you're lucky, you work in and around your Genius every day. If so, congratulations! If not, let's get you connected to the opportunities afforded by knowing, embracing, and implementing the incredibly expansive qualities associated with doing the one thing on the planet you were gifted to do.

But really, what the heck is genius? Well, let's start first with what it's not! Genius is *not* a profession. Never. Not ever. Genius is not your IQ results or your SAT score (even if you had a perfect score!), or your aptitude in science or math. It's not your ability to do Sudoku or complete the New York Times Sunday crossword puzzle fully.

Genius is a singular gift of super high-level talent, embedded into every fiber of your being—your DNA, if you will. You received this talent as "factory equipment" and it explains why siblings with the same two parents can be so radically different, in personality, yes, but also in terms of talents. One is the introverted, "computer type" and the other is the extroverted, artsy type. In simple terms, they were given completely different talents, and I would suggest, by design, and for a very specific reason.

Genius appears at the intersection of *beauty and power*, and in its purest form, creates a field of abundance and unlimited expansion, for those who choose to embrace it. Common descriptions of when you are playing in your Genius: "In the zone", "flow", and "effortless", or "feels like play". Genius is also quite attractional—people want to partner with, hire, and engage genius level talent...which means they want to hire, engage, and utilize *your* talent!

Attributes That Surround Genius

Have you ever noticed how some people seem to succeed without much stress, effort, or sweat, where others struggle in the same role or task? Chances are, one person is working in, around, and "through" their Genius, and the other is working through a methodology connected to training, process, skills, or competence. Both will get the job done. One will enjoy the process much more.

Why? Noting the attributes and characteristics that surround Genius helps to explain succinctly. Here are some of the notions that surround Genius:

Passion or joy – you *love* to do this, and could do it all day long, every day, and be very happy.

Effortless – in (and around) your Genius, results come

without much effort, as you hold the talent necessary for great success. It comes naturally.

Specificity of talent – Genius = a singular, high-level talent, not a role or job.

Continual improvement with use – in short, the more you engage and challenge your Genius, the more it improves. You begin to relish big challenges in your field of Genius, and expand possibilities.

An expansive playing field – although your talent is super specific, the playground or playing field to utilize and engage your Genius is incredibly abundant, and expands with use.

Well, how about areas where we have no Genius at all. Can we develop a genius level of talent?

For me, anything mechanical poses a great challenge. Given a simple "Saturday morning fix-it project", I end up at the hardware store three or four times, buying extra tools to correct the secondary mess made by having little aptitude, energy, or intuition as to how to change a washer on a leaky faucet. Invariably, after spending obscene amounts of money to change out a $0.50 washer, I call a plumber to fix the pipe I broke, fix the hole in the sheetrock, and the water damage caused by breaking a pipe and poking a hole in the wall.

Could I learn to do this project correctly? Yes. Will I ever possess genius-level talent in this realm? Never. That does not make me any less of a human being, just not the guy to help with the installation of your new deck or kitchen counter tops. I'll make sandwiches and lemonade when it comes to contributing to that project.

I was raised by an automotive engineer who routinely built additions and remodels of our family home, simply by working on weekends. No formal plans. No additional tools. No trade specialists hired. He loved to do this, was very capable, and seemed happiest when adding utility and value to our family home. Different guy, different talent. He is my Dad, and that makes little difference in what talents he possesses and what talents I possess. We got what we got in terms of Genius.

Is it any wonder that he gravitated to the field of designing engines? The two (home construction and auto engineering) are connected well enough, and although I never knew my Dad's exact genius, I did know it showed up in and around mechanical things.

And just in case you're curious, no gender holds any particular talent dictated by societal norms. For example, women are not confined to super high level talent that would lead to having or raising children, organizing, scheduling, or running a bake sale. Nor would men be limited to fixing or building things with their hands, hunting, or leadership. A talent is a talent, and devoid of any gender biases.

The 3 Components of a Genius Statement

A "Genius statement" outlines your entire Genius, and holds three components:

WHAT – the simplest gift of talent, spoken as an action. This is the raw, powerful, and beautiful talent you were given at birth. You cannot change WHAT you got. It also = WHAT you give/do for others. It sounds like this: "My Genius is doing this specific activity..."

HOW – this is the unique methodology you have developed, honed, and refined over the course of your lifetime. It = HOW you do WHAT you do. In the age old conversation of "nature and nurture" your HOW falls almost entirely into the "nurture" camp. Your entire lifetime, perhaps by design, has been the playground for developing your unique delivery of your high level talent. Your HOW sounds like this "....I do this by Step 1, Step 2, and Step 3."

WHY – You received a great gift of talent, and have spent a lifetime developing it. Ever consider that you might have been given this talent (as opposed to another) for a specific reason? In its simplest form, your WHY = your purpose on the planet—the reason you exist. Other than that, it does not have much use at all. Your WHY sounds like this: "I do this, because I believe ...."

Here is what a complete Genius statement sounds like. This is my own Genius.

"My Genius is creating seemingly impossible outcomes, that address multiple, diverse objectives. (My WHAT) I do this by designing one unifying game (Step 1), enrolling all of the participants (Step 2), and then constantly adjusting the game to insure that each player gets exactly what they came for (Step 3). (My HOW) I do this because I believe that everyone deserves to win BIG! (My WHY)"

Could I have found or created this statement online, or by taking one of the many really good, eerily accurate personality or assessment tests? I suggest not. Genius is way too highly specific. It contains *your* language. The articulation of the specific talent does not come for a drop down list of possibilities that you choose. It comes from an expressive process of you outlining episodes of peak performance—where your WHAT, HOW, and WHY were all fully aligned.

You have had episodes where these three elements have all been in place at one time. The trick is, you may or may not have recognized that you were in the presence of your Genius, so our tendency as human beings is to dismiss these episodes as good fortune, dumb luck, the result of other people's contributions, or a myriad of other explanations for great results occurring.

Truth is, when placed in the presence of your Genius, you have no equal on the planet, and you will produce fabulous results every time, *even if* the challenge increases every time. There is no ceiling on the level of your talent. You simply have to know what it is, and then place yourself in the arenas where your specific Genius is needed and wanted most.

There's a wise saying with regards to money, and it applies to Genius as well: "Money goes to where it is needed most, and stays where it is treated best." Genius works the same way. Go to where your Genius will be needed most, and stay in the arenas where it is treated best!

Particularly, as it relates to the WHY part of your Genius statement, expanding your life's contribution, joy, play, and happiness will be directly proportional to the amount of time your invest in activities closely connected to your life's purpose, your WHY, if you will. Even if you are not in your highest talent, when you are working in conjunction with your life's purpose, almost any form of activity has high meaning.

Go to where your purpose, or WHY, is treated best!

So What the Heck is *My* Unique Genius?

You have a Genius. You are a Genius. So how do you find it, how do you know it's right, and how do your design your life to take advantage of it?

All great (and fair) questions.

In working with over 7,500 clients in the pursuit of discovering their highest level, unique talent, I have learned that your Genius cannot be "concocted" or discovered with a formula, an online test, or by picking and choosing components that feel or sound right. We all possess blind spots as human beings, and we all project our desires or wishes when learning about ourselves. If we are allowed to simply choose what we think might be our Genius, there is a chance we could get it right...but more often than not, we simply choose what looks most needed, wanted, or wished for, rather than what is actually present.

The methodology for uncovering or discovering your Genius is simple. It can take about two hours, and it is very accurate. Why? Because it involves a series of stories you are led to "uncover" from your history, that fit a specific pattern where your WHAT (your high level talent), your HOW (your unique way of producing results in that talent) and your WHY (your most fundamental core belief) all align. How many of these stories do you have? Probably dozens. For my clients, I seek four or five in order to see the clear patterns that show up around you, when your WHAT, HOW, and WHY are all aligned.

What has shown up in cases where these three key elements exist simultaneously is a clearly surprising result which occurred at the time. The result will look surprising to *you*, predictable to others around you, once you can recognize, own, and then duplicate the criteria needed for that talent to expand and flourish.

Sounds simple, and in many ways, it is. The hardest part is not figuring it out. Sadly, the surprisingly difficult part is that even after discovering their individual, unique Genius, many people simply cannot *own* the power and beauty contained in their talent, so they never put it to full use. Occasionally, they will have peak episodes, and that will be due to random interactions with their Genius, rather than a full strategic employment of their greatest gift of talent.

What might this look like? In my case, I thrive in arenas where there is little or no chance of success—long shots, if you will. That atmosphere simply arouses my talent, and gives notice that it is time to play—expansion, if you will, of a sleeping or latent talent.

Once there is a "seemingly impossible outcome" or long shot, then everything else kicks in, and I am off to the races. More often than not, we (all involved) create a big success where there was no clear possibility prior. In short, everyone wins, which is why I play in the first place—my WHY.

As mentioned, though, your Genius will not come from a formula, a test, or reading, researching, or interviewing others. It can only come from your own experiences, and will contain your own words.

The Dirty Little Secret about Genius and Expansion

Genius is not for everyone. Just ask an "average" person. Discovering your Genius is really fun. Owning it fully takes some courage—the courage to lead a great life—a life utilizing your greatest gift of talent. Your life then will expand in relation to the contribution you can make, the impact you can have, and the joy you will give and receive as a part of living the expansive life of Genius.

Dyana is a good friend who discovered her Genius. Dyana's Genius is "I champion the unique gifts of others so that they may claim their own divinity," (her HOW omitted by choice), because she fundamentally believes that we are all connected. Can you guess at what she did for a career? Minister? Nope, she's an atheist. Therapist? Nope. She runs (or ran) her own executive search firm. A "head hunter", if you will! 100 percent commission, lots of hustle, super capitalistic, and with a Genius that was wholly spiritual!

If you think about it, Dyana's Genius would be a great way to do effective head hunting (okay, "executive search") because she would have the natural talent to make sure that the candidates were great fits for the culture they were being hired into, and vice versa for the firms she placed people into. She was good at what she did...and also realized that once she started to *own* her Genius, her contribution and calling were not as well served by her career choice, as perhaps doing something more meaningful. In short, her last executive search would be for herself.

Problem was, Dyana only knew that executive search was not her *calling*—just a pretty good fit for her high level talent of connecting people with their own divinity. Here's where the expansion fit, and it will for you too. Like you, Dyana took the courageous step to live the fully expansive life connected to her Genius, rather than using her Genius as best she could in what she was doing. She made the decision to invest the rest of her life into a career/calling that would take much better advantage of her high level talent, yes, but would also connect perfectly with her WHY. Dyana sold her executive search firm, and had enough funds to transition for a year into coaching. She did much training and certification, and her talents fit naturally into the field she chose.

The "trick" is that Dyana took had the courage to pursue an expansive field, a place where she could contribute (and receive) much more than what she had been doing.

Does this mean you need to change careers, in order to *own* your Genius? Not at all. The courage to redesign how you take on your career, or your volunteer opportunities, or the way you relate to friends and family is the same courage Dyana employed to redesign her career. It's a simple, powerful, courageous choice to live the most expansive life you can live. The rewards pay off for the rest of your life!

I'll get you started on the path. If you're reading this book, you're clearly interested in expansion, and living a great life. The question is, are you interested in action? If this is compelling for you now, go to evokinggenius.com, register, and I will send you free videos to get you started on your own journey into the expansive life of Genius.

All the best!

ABOUT THE AUTHOR: JOHN HITTLER

"How were you able to pull *that* off?"

This question follows John a lot, in his professional, personal, and charitable endeavors. John specializes in *creating seemingly impossible outcomes*, whether transforming a struggling team to become the top performer, or engaging an audience with his playful, interactive, life-changing style. His belief is simple: we are each endowed with one *unique* genius, different than any other person on the planet. John uses his genius to create seemingly impossible outcomes and in doing so, helps people win big!

Professionally, John partners with clients to create outcomes that they simply could not imagine possible, through an encouraging coaching style. "The clients always set the agenda," says John, "and my job is to make the process of lasting behavior change or transformation safer and more attractive than standing still." That result comes about often in a playful manner, transforming work into play, and unleashing individual, team, and organizational "genius" in the process.

John runs **Evoking Genius**, a transformational business coaching company. "We take struggling teams and help them to transform into top performers. We take already great teams and partner with them to break through to the next highest level. That almost always centers upon releasing the pent up talent in each individual and team. That sounds simple, and it's not always easy. Our job is to make that process accessible, attractive, and mostly...safe. It never hurts to make it fun too," claims John, who spent more than his fair share of time in the principal's office for his playful approach to life. That same approach makes transformation much more appealing for clients.

After earning a bachelor's degree in Economics and German from Georgetown University, John quickly found the entrepreneurial path much to his liking, starting 9 companies and one charitable foundation, all in different markets, ranging from catering to medical devices over a 20 year span. He now centers most of his energy on his coaching practice, as it fits both his genius and his passion to help others win big! He speaks to numerous Fortune 1000 teams and organizations, and also enjoys working with smaller entrepreneurs in EO (Entrepreneurs Organization) and YPO (Young Presidents Organization). John still sits on several charitable boards, mostly in the area of eliminating child poverty and human trafficking. Giving back is simply part of his personal ethic. In his private life, John is father of seven, three of whom are adopted orphans, and that same ethic of creating unity from diverse cultures rules in the family. "My 7 kids have six different sets of DNA, with only two sharing the same biological parents. We are one family, and we all get along because we share one common vision together—to care for and nurture each other's growth and success." That simple approach spills over into everything he touches—to create "big wins" for people by working together for one agreed upon goal.

When not working, John can be found at a CrossFit affiliate, keeping ultra-fit and competing in local, regional, and national fitness competitions. His trademark pasty white legs are easily spotted among the participants. John also loves to cook, especially for close friends and family. "Food is love", says John frequently. "There is always room for one more special guest at the dinner table in our home. That one last person is usually the one who needed to be included the most."
You can find John at evokinggenius.com.

Chapter 9

Unleash the Inner "Money Goddess" in You

By Arlene M. Broussard

What if, regardless of your career, you always have enough? What if you knew a sure way that didn't take a lot of time each month, but rewarded you with financial abundance after doing this practice? What if you could do work that you enjoy and command enough wealth for an abundant life? Many of us struggle with money. We weren't taught how to manage money in school and many of our parents didn't teach us this because they didn't know how to themselves or because they were so busy raising the family they didn't have time.

Given this lack of money education and the negative perception around wealth, we sometimes doubt our own ability to manage it well. We operate from a place of fear and avoidance. But it doesn't have to be this way. Once you become aware that you can control your outlook by filling your mind with the beliefs of a money management maven, you too can expand in this area of your life.

That you are reading this book is evidence that you already know on some level how to use your mind to create and improve your life experience. What I'm going to share is how I used the energy of expansion to amass $1 Million.

My story is unique and common at the same time. It's unique in that I didn't learn what I know from a money expert or from my parents in a traditional way. What's common about it is that the underlying method I used is based on the laws of goal setting and expansion.

The philosophy of "What you focus on expands" is key to transforming your financial life.

I met my ex-husband when I was in my last year of college, full of hope. After several years of what appeared to be a happy marriage, we just wouldn't work through our differences. Our marriage painfully ended. Throughout our relationship we thought we were managing our money just fine. Then we sat down with our divorce attorney to calculate what she called our "financial net worth" – boy did we get a surprise. We learned that while having a small financial net worth and no children gifted us with nothing to argue over, it also left us both with very little savings. This was the first I had even considered a need to know what my financial net worth was or even how to calculate it. I was frankly in shock.

No house, no nest egg, no job, and a very broken spirit. I realize now that we had not chosen to be wealthy or accumulate any specific amount of money.

So I moved in with my Mom. During this time, I felt confused and lost. My friends, while well meaning in their attempts, were not giving me the right kind of support I needed to get me out of the abyss. I was floating in numbness, with no direction. And then I noticed something about my grandmother. She prayed every morning and attended church every Sunday. So I started attending church with her and my mom. Slowly and miraculously, week-by-week, I was finding more and more relief. I was changing the thoughts in my head to those of a beautiful, joyful place where I regained my peace. From this higher energy state, I was able to start out on my journey of finding work. And when I was finally in the process of securing a job, I learned I had a glass ceiling in my head.

How does one break through our own glass ceiling about money? And how much salary is enough?

When I was offered this first job after my divorce...my new boss asked me my salary requirement. I told him a number that was 10% more than I was making in my last job. He paid me 30 percent more. (I became a statistic in that moment: this is one reason why women make $0.77 to the $1 of men.) I didn't ask for enough. I had not dreamed I could make that much. I didn't know what jobs like that paid. I was limited by my own experience and my negative beliefs about money.

Know that you are worthy of financial abundance.

It was the blessing of a fair boss that shifted my perspective on how much I can earn. Wow. What a lesson in expansion for me! As my paychecks started coming in, I realized I didn't have my ex-husband to figure out the money with me. So I started looking online and in books about money management. I kicked around in my head and researched "how much money is enough to retire on". Then I discussed it with my brother, Stephen, and decided that $500,000 plus was a good target for me, a single woman living in Los Angeles.

My next step was to set up a spreadsheet on the computer to track my net worth. I laid out my assets and liabilities and set up the formulas to calculate my net worth on a quarterly basis. All right! I was on my way.

Set up tools to measure your success.

After setting up that first tool, I realized I also needed a second tool. I recalled that I had received one very important lesson about money from my Mom when I was a child. She tallied her monthly bills on the inside of a manila folder. The few times I observed her doing this, it didn't occur to me what she was doing. My money consciousness at the time was receiving nickels and dimes for chores and then using them to buy ice cream at Thrifty's down the street. Fortunately, once I was an adult facing my own financial crisis, that lesson proved to be very helpful and inspired me to create a second measurement tool. Thanks, Mom!

Pay attention to the guidance you receive.

That manila folder of monthly expenses that my Mom created out of necessity sparked my realization that I needed to track my monthly expenses. So I set up my second tool: a spreadsheet that added all my monthly income and subtracted all my expenses. I also saved all of my receipts and loaded them into this monthly net income spreadsheet every week or two as I had accumulated a pile of receipts.

Small shifts in your habits affect your financial net worth.

These actions became habits of my life and subconsciously guided my spending choices. Whenever it came time to make a purchase, I knew I would be logging it into my net income spreadsheet and that it would affect my financial net worth. It made me very aware of spending money on wants versus needs. I didn't deprive myself, but I didn't over extend myself either.

The next Christmas, my cousin Anthony who was in his last months of a long struggle with cancer, gave me a silver plated million-dollar paperweight for Christmas. I know this gift was his way of telling me he had confidence I would one day have a million dollars. Anthony knew me well: we were very close and I spent a lot of time with him through his illness up to the day of his transition to the nonphysical. You see, Anthony was more than my cousin. My Mom and

Grandparents raised Anthony and his brother in the house with us because their parents were not able to raise them. So we were more like brother and sister. And that he believed in me meant there must be some truth to this.

Goal setting fundamental: set a target. *(Or have your cousin set it for you.)*

That gift from Anthony caused me to double my goal to $1 Million of financial net worth. My subconscious mind went on to work wonderfully. Whatever I was feeding my mind, was what grew. And I fed it the belief that I would have $1 Million. So my silver plated million-dollar paper weight (my new target) really did it for me. I continued my habit of saving my receipts, tracking my net worth and logging my expenses. Plugging away, living my life, ups and downs, joys and pains. Until one day, I proved that what I had been focusing on, my financial net worth truly had been expanding. I had accumulated $1,037,420.

Eureka! I had achieved my goal!

I was really doing it! And of course in addition to my cousin Anthony, there were other people around me channeling spirit, guiding me along the way. My boss at the time said, "Why aren't you creating more success? You have so much potential." And my mentor and closest friend both told me, "Arlene, you can do whatever you set your mind to; you always do." Surely, this is true for all of us. I am not unique in this aspect of my life: we can all do most of what we set our minds to. It comes down to choice and focus: what we repeatedly think about. And truly it is in the pursuit of our dreams that we find joy. The end result is nice but not the place that my fulfillment came from. It was during the journey of setting a goal and tracking to that goal on a weekly, quarterly, and yearly basis, that my confidence grew.

I had all these limitations in my mind about my history. When I was one-year-old my father was diagnosed with mental illness. As a result, growing up, I had an underlying fear that I was not good enough. I would not push myself too hard in any area for fear that I would reach my breaking point with stress and have a mental or emotional breakdown like my dad. I believed that life as I was living it, "playing small", was adequate – I wasn't good enough to be a millionaire anyway! I didn't come from one of *those* families: one of those families with a mom and a dad with a good paying job and a house with a white picket fence.

Everyone has fear: take the fear and move forward anyway.

Why I was able to break through my fear and go for it anyway can be summarized into three basic elements: my outlook, my habits, and my measuring what I had. Becoming expert at this, unleashing my inner "money goddess", I amassed a financial net worth of $1 Million dollars. And what now? I feel at ease, I feel inspired, I feel like I can do what I feel called to do next. What I focus on expands. I focused on my goal of $500,000 and then $1 Million. Not every day consciously, but every couple of weeks. And subconsciously, when I considered making purchases, I had my goal in mind, and I did not spend frivolously. I purchased what I needed. I was generous with my money, but not at the expense of my goal. I had chosen to become a millionaire.

I had friends telling me, "You should buy a house, the market is ripe." This was the couple of years leading up to the housing market bubble in 2007. Something in me knew that wasn't right for me at the time. I valued experiences, nature, people, and spirit: I didn't need a house for any of that. So I didn't buy. And when the housing market dropped, I had $400,000 in cash. And I felt secure. What's that about? It's about trusting the guidance I receive. Trusting that I will know in my body what is right for me as long as I nurture my relationship with God, with divinity. This is what I know about money expansion.

Listen to the guidance you receive: pay attention to your body.

I openly share this gift of what I have learned. I am dedicated to helping others create a better relationship with money: to set a financial goal and to track their expenses and their financial net worth so they too can be a maven of money management and create the wealth they desire. What you focus on truly expands.

Some might say, *but you didn't enjoy life*. Not true. I traveled all over the United States with work putting on face-to-face events for corporations. I travelled to Germany, Italy, Mexico, Switzerland, Japan, Brazil, China, Israel and Egypt sometimes for work and sometimes on vacation. I went scuba diving in Thailand and the Red Sea off the Sinai Peninsula of Egypt. I enjoyed a wonderful relationship with my boyfriend. I spent great time with my immediate family. Was it sometimes rocky? Sure? But what is life if not a colorful contrast of ups and downs. Did challenging things happen to me along the way? Yes, I experienced tremendous loss to cancer, to drugs, and to side effects of mental illness and bouts of depression. These have been tender and difficult times. My life is not without complications, but it is full and joyful and abundant because of these steps that I took to create financial abundance for myself. At the end of this particular $1 Million wealth-building journey, I realized that there really is no true security in money or anything else material. Lasting peace only comes from my nurtured connection with divinity. I know I could lose all my money in a moment. But it sure feels good to know that I am a millionaire right now, and that should I ever choose to create this kind of wealth again, I know I can. I have mastered the three elements: o̲utlook, h̲abits, and m̲easurement (ohm).

You can, too! So choose your target and let's get started to amassing your wealth!

ABOUT THE AUTHOR: ARLENE BROUSSARD

Arlene is an expert in demystifying money. Her mission is empowering women to activate their inner "money goddess" to create wealth regardless of what they may be facing in their personal lives.

While a student at the Anderson School of Management at UCLA, she struggled with thoughts of not being good enough to understand the workings of Wall Street and money. Arlene went on to amass more than $1 Million after learning that there are three unchangeable elements to creating wealth regardless of your life story: Outlook, Habits, and Measurement. She now teaches this through easy to follow products and services live and online.

Her goal: to empower millions of women to be a maven of money management and create the wealth they desire. Find out more at www.ArleneBroussard.com.

Chapter 10

Expanding Life After Loss
By Lisette Broussard

From my experience of losing my brother, who was a young 21, and then my father, who was a young 53, to cancer, I have learned to connect to them in spirit. This has enriched my life in so many ways. It has been a long road that started with pain, then acceptance and ultimately enlightenment and expansion that I hope to share with you so that you may find comfort sooner after losing loved ones.

Ultimately it is my goal to help those that are looking, to learn to connect energetically to those who have crossed over before us. This is not a religious document, however I believe religion has its place in personal expansion. For me, it is a spiritual enlightenment, and connection that I have honed and have fallen in love with. I live more from my soul, my inner-self, the part of me that is connected and one with everything else in a universe that works synergistically in our favor all the time. Forever.

My experience started when I was in my second year of college at the University of California Santa Barbara. College, I thought, was is supposed to be a time for fun and learning and growing. It was that in many ways, however, one day everything changed. I received a phone call from my mother that my younger brother, Marcus, who was a 17-year-old high school senior, was diagnosed with a serious type of cancer. He had a tumor in his hip the size of a grapefruit that was diagnosed as a high-grade chondrosarcoma.

I was heartbroken and I could hear the pain in my mother's voice as she told me. My brother Marcus was as positive as could be. He was such a light. Over the next year I traveled home to Sacramento often and saw my brother start his road to recovery. This consisted of a heavy treatment of chemotherapy and once the tumor shrunk to a manageable size he went in for surgery to have it removed.

I remember my parents doing everything in their power to find the right doctors who could cure my brother. They spent a lot of money getting several opinions from the best in the field, even flying as far as Texas to meet with a reputable surgeon. Marcus, an active teenager who played football and baseball for his high school team was very adamant about not losing his leg and ability to walk. This is when we learned about quality of life decisions. Of course we wanted him to do whatever it took to ensure that he would live, however Marcus operated from a different perspective. This was His life and he was passionate about living it without any physical restrictions. While most surgeons were recommending amputation, it seemed like a miracle when my parents met Dr. James Johnston, an orthopedic surgeon at The University of California San Francisco. He proposed surgery using a new technology that would allow Marcus to keep his hip and leg attached and with function.

I flew in for the surgery and remember sitting with my family in the waiting room for 14 terrifying hours during the procedure. Marcus underwent a total hip replacement and his left pelvis was rebuilt with medical bone cement. It was scary and sad but he came out of it and did great. Dr. Johnston was able to get good margins and my brother was able to keep his hip and leg intact. In fact, the surgeon later called Marcus his golden child and used his case to teach others. Marcus began his recovery and remission. He got back to his normal young adult life with his same enthusiasm for life that had always remained with him pre-cancer and post. I remember Marcus showing off his surgical staples with pride, he had over 1000. He even started giving them to friends as souvenirs.

Two years later, my brother started to feel pain and it was soon learned that the cancer had returned. I had just graduated from college and moved back home to be near my family. It was explained to us, that if the cancer were to come back it would be much more aggressive and the prognosis would not be great. We watched my brother get sick all over again, however his spirits always remained lifted. He was so positive, even as his body started to deteriorate. It was clear that Marcus developed an acceptance and even a connection to dying. As a family we wanted to try anything and everything to fight. It wasn't that he wasn't a fighter, however on the contrary he had a very peaceful presence around the outcome. "It is time for me to go home" are words I remember him speaking and at the time not realizing what he meant. Over time we accepted that he was passing. I remember the night before he died, he had gone into the hospital with renal failure earlier that week and we finally told him it was ok, we were going to let him go. We expressed our love and said our goodbyes and shortly after that he became unconscious. He passed away that night very peacefully. It was as if he was waiting for us to come into acceptance so he could make his transition. And that he did. In fact, my mother said that when the time came he took one last breath and held his hands up towards the sky as if he were reaching for something. I wish I was there, but I was too scared to stay.

After this experience, I was derailed. It seemed so unfair that such a good person could die so young. At the same time I wanted to understand how he could be so peaceful with it. This began my pursuit of figuring life out and ultimately my own expansion from human physical awareness to a knowing of the non-physical spiritual world.

I have spent the last 12 years reading and researching everything I could get my hands on about life, death and spirituality. I have learned from amazing teachers such as Dr. Raymond Moody, Danion Brinkley, Neale Donald Walsch, Abraham through Esther Hicks, Deepak Chopra, Louise Hay, and so many more. I have learned to have a personal relationship with my higher power and to connect with the non-physical pure positive energetic life that is available to us all. I have learned about the Universal laws of attraction. The best I can explain it is that before the experience of losing my brother, I believed I was happy, and I was, but after the experience and learning how to connect with my spirit I started to live on a whole other plane. It is like I was blind and now I can see.

My whole family awakened spiritually and my father, Michael, had a mystical experience where he felt compelled to write a book about life and the purpose of. He felt it was a calling. The title of his book was Clear. He spoke of tapping into an energy where everything in the universe seemed clear and everything flowed synergistically. He spoke of the five elements that made up human life: Spirituality, Energy, Clarity, Reality and Fantasy. And how, with an understanding of these, we can live happier more expanded lives. He wrote of the need for everyone in our world to cultivate Love and to spread positive energy. This would bring about the new age of heaven on Earth. My dad and I collaborated often on our thoughts about life and spirituality. Our conversations took me out of this world. Into an expanded universe that was right here in our grasp. It was truly phenomenal. My father was writing his book for eight years, and could only write when he was "clear". He felt that the information was coming from something more than him; a higher power was using him as an instrument to get the message out. Eight years into writing the book, that got to be over 300 pages long... he got stuck on the last chapter. It was about healing. My dad started to feel sick and lethargic which we all thought was the flu at first. After one week and no relief and my mother constantly pressuring him to get it checked out, he went to the doctor.

My father, Michael, fell acutely sick and learned that he had colon cancer stage IV that had metastasized to his liver. He was a very active 53-year-old, played basketball every weekend since he was a young teenager so this was a shock to us all. Apparently he was asymptomatic which is how it went undiscovered for so long. He was diagnosed in November 2013 and passed away a little over one month later on December 20th.

His oncologist from the very beginning told us he did not have much time and that he was very sick. Life was putting all that we had learned to a test. I shall boldly say my Dad and I passed. Despite the negative information we were receiving from specialists, we stayed in positive sprits. He had grown a rather large following on Facebook with his positive messages from his book and he took the opportunity to share his cancer experience with everyone. The support and amount of positive energy that he cultivated on his Facebook page was amazing. He connected with so many on a level that seemed superhuman. That last month with him was such a positive presence, we connected as we always did despite the news he was very ill. Because we understood death as a transition we did not waste time, but just the opposite, we relished in the time we had. We loved, and laughed and told stories. As my dad grew sicker he went into comfort care in the hospital. This time around I was not scared. I stayed with my dad along side my mom until the end, or rather until his transition.

The feeling of peace in the room immediately after his passing was indescribable. There really is an energy and a presence when one leaves their physical body. I can honestly say that I did not experience loss this time around but an energetic connection. In the immediate days and weeks after his passing it was like I could communicate with him, and he was helping me out in unfathomable ways. My sales sky rocketed during a time that is usually slow for me. My life felt as if I was walking on a red carpet, everything I wanted and needed was in my reach instantly no matter how unrealistic it seemed. My brilliant Dad had taken on a new form that seemed to have a lot more influence. I was in an amazing, peaceful, gracious space with his spirit and with life. I was experiencing what he wrote about. I was Clear.

It's been an amazing journey and I am finding after practicing staying in this state, by meditation, exercising and loving others, I am able to connect to the greater part of myself and to those who have gone before me. It is an amazing existence to live in and I feel called to share it with those experiencing loss. I have a deep desire to help people experience connection as I have experienced it.

Life is unbelievably good if we open our eyes to it. If we let Love and Positive Energy in we can live a heaven on Earth Expanded Life. We truly are in a time of expanding awareness. This is an amazing time to be alive. We are eternal and we are all a part of one big entity. All connected, in our physical form and in our even greater non-physical form, our spirit.

Wisdom from my Dad, Michael Anthony Broussard...

The Alpha Elements

To explain and solve matters we often view as complex using my "Alpha Elements" seems easily done once the quintessence of each member element is understood. **Spirituality** is the purest essence of us all. We are of spirit. The spirit is also known as the soul. And, it is sometimes referred to as the self and the inner-self too. **Energy** is the force through which our spirit interacts with existence. And our earthly existence consists of all persons, places and things we know today. **Clarity** is truth and is personal.

Clarity allows us to draw upon a strong and immeasurably powerful spiritual relationship with God to know the true importance of all we do and all that is done to us. **Reality** consists of simply all of the persons, places and things that exist in our world. Reality is tangible, calculable, and definable. **Fantasy** is comprised of all that we seek in life to shape our spirits in our own way; a right that is divinely given to us by God. The fact that Fantasy exists insures that no spirit will be perfectly shaped while living on Earth. Not perfectly shaped, but no need to fret, as only God can be perfect anyway.

Good (Positive) Energy

Good Energy and positive Energy are one in the same. When I speak of either, I am speaking of the other too. It is impossible to deny the presence of good Energy. We all have experienced it and sincerely felt it. We have come to know our emotions as the measuring stick of Energy. Good Energy is processed by our minds and our bodies in the form of laughter, smiles, encouragement, warm hugs and kisses on the cheek to name a few.

The presence of good Energy makes our world a livable place. We live to feel good! When we cease to feel good often enough, we can become saddled with depression. Life then becomes to us a heavy load. We usually can find others, typically in the form of friends and loved ones, to throw us a life preserver and pull us to safety. A very good aspect of good Energy is that it can be shared. And transferred even. Where our Spirituality is concerned, this is a powerful mechanism. We use this power everyday, and yet we rarely think of it justly. In perhaps an unconscious quest to be like God, an abundance of individual good Energy serves us best. We become greedy for good Energy just like God is. But we are not God, and understanding this is crucial to playing God's game of Life on Earth. We are to create good Energy in the most massive amounts. Not hoard it for ourselves. God is not an individual spirit. God is all spirits combined. Only when we realize that we can only become like God by collectively creating good Energy, will we approach winning this divine game we know as Life on Earth.

In Science, the 1st Law of Thermodynamics states that MATTER can neither be created nor destroyed. Consequently, nothing that consists of MATTER ever DIES. It may be TRANSFORMED to another state of EXISTENCE, but technically it is still MATTER. Fortunately SINS, TRANSGRESSIONS and HATE are NOT MATTER and these CAN DIE if we LEARN HOW TO and THEN let them. SINCERITY, KINDNESS and LOVE are NOT MATTER either, but I surmise that these CANNOT DIE. They can be unappreciated and ignored only to be rejuvenated once again. Our SPIRITS are perhaps the most valuable gift. Technically SPIRITS are not MATTER. But SPIRITS may MATTER the very most of all. So allow me to blend Science and the Metaphysical to update the 1st Law of Thermodynamics - "MATTER and ALL THAT MATTERS can neither be created nor destroyed (by MAN)". There. I did it. Can I get away with that? **~Mikesay**

ABOUT THE AUTHOR: LISETTE BROUSSARD

Lisette Broussard lives in San Diego, CA. In her professional life she has a fascinating career in medical device sales. She loves being a part of a team that helps patients achieve the best possible surgical outcomes. In her personal life she discovered her passion for learning about life, death and spirituality after losing her brother at a young age to cancer.

His transition inspired her to learn more about the spiritual non-physical world that she felt was within our Earthly reach. She has spent the past 12 years researching the subject and learned how to tune in to her spirit through practices such as meditation, hypnotherapy and Reiki energetic healing.

She found that she could connect with her inner self, the part of herself that was purely positive and bring about quick changes to her outer circumstances in her favor. It was clear that she had expanded as a spiritual being when she was able to connect with her father after he passed away with cancer. She did not feel loss at the time of his passing or after, but on the contrary felt extremely connected with him and his wisdom. She feels that it is her mission to help others deal with the loss of their loved ones and move forward in a more spiritually connected way.

Chapter 11

The Courage to Live your Greatest Expansion

By Connie Viveros

Many of us are drawn to the idea of our own expansion, of living an expanded life, of being more, of being in alignment with our highest selves and our fullest expression. But how do we do that? For me, the true source of living an expanded life is knowing how to open up to love, and living life with a wide open heart, over and over and over again, regardless of the circumstances around me.

My own journey of spiritual awakening began over three decades ago, and from everything I have gathered, read, personally experienced or taught to others, for me it comes down to one basic understanding: once I commit to my own awakening, my *self* will awaken, and that awakening self is ever-evolving and always expanding. I may or may not be aware of the subtle impulses or manifestations of that awakening, but I trust that I am always in forward motion. Even when I cannot see where I am headed, I can energetically feel myself moving forward, in the right direction. I am more comfortable than ever not knowing where I am headed, because I trust life's mystery unfolding around me and in me, participating in the expansion of not only myself but also of the unfolding collective consciousness.

Of course, when I am 'awake' to this ever-expanding energy working inside of me, my experience becomes far more enjoyable than when I am not consciously aligning myself with my own expansion. But that's the beauty of choice, isn't it? Each of us gets to decide just how consciously we want to participate in our own awakening. Yay, right? But let me get back to my own journey.

When I examine my life, I see that it has been a story about interacting with fear – fighting with it, being overwhelmed, defeated, and outraged by it. Fear has come in predictable forms, such as desperately low self esteem as a child; or in sudden shocking ways, such as traumatized reactions and startling phobias. It has washed over me in waves, piercing my heart like a dagger, and at times choked my breathing. I've endured periods of intense fear about my lovability, employability, my intelligence, financial security, and even my weight!

Fear has dared and tested me, and repeatedly confronting it has altered the arc and scope of my existence into something more expansive and satisfying than I ever expected. It has certainly propelled me onto the spiritual path and has revealed itself as my most profound and uncompromising teacher. I was an exceptionally weak child – skinny and afraid, confused and always feeling I lagged behind others. Being the youngest of five children growing up in the 1960s often translated into not being good enough – certainly not as good as my brothers and sister--not pretty enough, smart enough and certainly not lovable enough, if at all. I felt like a complete failure.

In my early teens I turned to drugs and alcohol to escape the horror of being me. Hiding became something I did well for many years. As I got older, instead of taking drugs I hid behind various lifestyles, beliefs and viewpoints. My fear resulted in foolish career choices, unhappy relationships, and unexplored opportunities. I tried to escape my fears in different ways, hoping to banish them by becoming a bartender; running away to live in Hawaii, Oregon; and burying myself in partying and unconscious behaviors –all in an effort to escape and hide from myself.

In the middle of all that running, I got my first nudge toward awakening in a class I was taking while attending college in Hawaii. It was an advanced Psychology course, and we were studying a unit called "alternative psychologies." The professor brought two guest speakers into class one day, Usha and Light, (obviously names gifted from their own spiritual awakening). They talked about a course they were studying called *"A Course in Miracles."* They invited everyone in class to attend a weekend seminar where we would experience something called "a rebirthing, or spiritual awakening." Being the young skeptics that we were, my friend and I decided to give it a try, and off we went.

On Friday night the facilitator gave each of us a white index card and asked us to write the answer to the question, "What would you like to have happen as a result of your time with us this weekend?" Already in disbelief at what they had shared with us, I wrote, "to have my entire belief system changed." I had grown up Catholic, so this seemed like a tall order!

Then came Sunday night, and to my utter amazement, when I read my little white index card, I had gotten exactly what I had asked for. I had been altered and changed at the deepest level of my understanding at that time in my life. It may sound crazy, but both my friend and I experienced a profound shift, although we could not explain it at the time. Everything seemed different. Doing perfectly ordinary things –watching television, eating ice cream, drinking water –felt extraordinary. That weekend was the beginning of my spiritual awakening.

I spent the next several months feeling alive in a way I had never known. Everything around me felt vibrant, and this vibrancy felt blissful. I was living in ecstasy, without the use of any drugs! I believe that in those days my soul reentered my body and my life force was returned to me, stronger and clearer than ever. That weekend that my friend and I had attended on a lark shifted my awareness forever. It was a turning point in my own evolution, like pushing a restart button that allowed me to step in to the fullness of my life. I expanded my energy to where I reengaged with my life through some sort of ecstasy. From that point forward, I began to feel led by something greater than myself.

With a new belief system in place, my life took on new disciplines, and a consistent spiritual practice began to change my everyday experience. A mysterious sort of congruency with my inner and outer experiences initiated with regularity. I began having visions, and encounters with light energies, water and plants. Everything around me seemed enlivened, and I could actually "see" the energy bodies of people, plants, and things!

When I began living in a state of open awareness, these two worlds – the physical world and the spiritual or energy world – inextricably began to align. In other words, my experience exemplified what I consider to be a spiritual truth – when you make a commitment to a spiritual path and honor it as best you can, the road rises up to meet you. After a while the path seems to deepen all on its own, and your experience begins to unfold with a kind of integrity and grace; the people you meet, the events that transpire, and the things you do all seem to be a part of a larger, more profound story. It's one that you are not quite aware is being told. It's the story of your life, and like any good story, nothing is in there without being essential to the outcome. The only thing is, because each person's story is utterly unique, you can't look to anyone to interpret your story. And you can never flip to the last page to see how it will end. Believe me, I've tried!

From my vast experiences with dozens of spiritual disciplines, I've found it is much easier to expand my awareness when my heart is wide open. It is through the practice of opening up, expanding our spiritual energy centers so that we can touch and heal. Our fear – whether it is the sharpness of anger, the heaviness of delusion, the anguish of hatred, or the unconscious impulse to sabotage ourselves – can be transformed into love.

To do this, we must learn to cultivate more gentleness toward ourselves. We can begin by relaxing. For example, when you spot something you dislike about yourself, the tendency is to turn up the negative self-talk. I'm not suggesting that you replace it with positive self-talk; I'm suggesting that you drop self-talk as much as possible, and relax. When you're in the grip of any negative feeling – whether it's depression, anxiety or dread – try to stop talking to yourself about it. This includes that voice in your head saying things like, "I'll never get what I want" "If I had only done/said/thought differently, things would be better," "I'm a complete failure," blah blah blah. Instead, allow your awareness to drop away from your thoughts and into your body. You'll immediately sense some physical sensation. Pinpoint where the sensation is in your body. Such thoughts are always accompanied by a physical manifestation. Perhaps your shoulders are hunched up, or your belly is tight, your breathing is shallow. As soon as you notice where the tension is, focus on this area of your body and consciously send relaxation to this part of you. If this is not possible, try relaxing everything surrounding the area. In relaxation something quite wonderful begins to develop. Tenderness and warmth rise to the surface effortlessly.

As you relax, visualize yourself in your mind's eye and think for a moment about how hard you work to create happiness for yourself and others. Sometimes it works and sometimes it doesn't, but you keep trying. Appreciate yourself for all you do. It can be tempting to skip this step because it may seem awkward, even narcissistic, to wish yourself well in this simple way. But be assured that there are many benefits to practicing self-acceptance and honoring your wish to be happy, and at peace. You begin to feel deep compassion for yourself. As Buddha said, *"You can search throughout the entire universe for someone who is more deserving of your love and affection than you are yourself, and that person is not to be found anywhere. You yourself, as much as anybody in the entire universe deserve your love and affection."*

So allow yourself to wish for your own happiness. Say to yourself silently: "I am happy, joyous, and free. May I be at peace, may I be a source of healing to everyone." You will begin to feel a lightness inside of you. Allow this energy to swell up inside you. As you practice expanding your own energy you will begin to touch your own natural tenderness and start to extend it out in wider and wider circles: first to those closest to you, then to a friend, then to a stranger, to an enemy, and finally to all beings. The gentleness you extend toward yourself can now include others. When the heart is open, confident and capable of handling all of its emotions with tenderness and grace, it freely and gracefully extends this feeling to others.

Sometimes our hearts open spontaneously. This can occur not only when we see suffering, but also when we observe someone else's authentic happiness. When my husband first proposed to me, the woman sitting at the table next to us burst into tears before I did! The point is that as we expand and open our hearts, we naturally expand toward others in compassion.

The crazy mystery of opening our heart means giving up our ideas about how things ought to be and instead finding a way to connect with our tenderness and vulnerability over and over and over again. To expand ourselves means to open our heart to the mystery and magic of our soul's story, the one we are born to live. This takes courage. When we allow ourselves to open our hearts, we might experience the sensation that there is no assurance of safety, no control over the outcome. We might draw back, allowing fear to take over once again.

The truth is, the more I love – *my anger, my enemies, my darkness, my light, myself, and others* –the more my heart opens to love and the more I expand, as my edges get softened and my sense of self grows larger. And more courage is required. Where does one get this courage? I don't know, but something tells me it all goes back to that commitment to our own awakening. When we make a commitment to our own spiritual path, the Universe brings us what we need, including courage.

The place to start is with who you are already, and what you are experiencing right now. Being who you are is all that's required. Maybe my inabilities to toe the line, to fit in, to succeed in a conventional life were not such bad things after all. They helped pry open my heart with every disappointment, rejection, and sense of utter failure. Like I did some 30-plus years ago, you start with who you are, and the goal is self-discovery. I am still discovering new horizons and new parts of me, and am in awe of how the road continues to rise up to meet me.

Living with a sense of deep compassion and tenderness for ourselves creates the kind of love that can transform the world. It is based on freedom from prejudice; giving up on self-condemnation, criticism and judgments; and becoming immersed in a self-interest that will naturally expand the collective consciousness. To really expand, to really love, is to give up all expectations and instead rest in your deepest vulnerabilities, trusting that who you are, at your most genuine and authentic, is who you are supposed to be. Only as you can give that love to yourself can you open your heart more fully to the world.

There is tremendous power in love. It builds our capabilities. Like a mother being handed her newborn child, connecting with our own souls awakens a fierceness and a deep, endless tenderness that is inseparable from each other, and growing with time as we call on both to nurture our charge. A devoted mother would do anything to protect her precious cargo, even superhuman acts in times of crisis. Rooted in powerful, tender love, the wellspring of her devotion allows for her child's perfect, expansive unfolding. When we can bring this devotion to our own expansion, with tenderness, power, and love, we start to relax in the fullness of who we are in the moment.

As you undertake your own practice of expansion, let me offer some advice. A meditation practice can have enormous benefits for opening your heart and expanding your energy. It creates new ways of relating to yourself, to your relationships and your life. If you do decide to take on a heart-opening practice, know that the way you see yourself will change, as will the way others see you. It may not happen right away, but in time it will. Are you prepared for things to change, and what that might be asked of you? Are you willing to be honest with yourself? An ongoing meditation practice will put you in touch with powerful energies. If you keep up a dedicated practice, these energies can be very supportive. If you decide a more casual practice is right for you, there may appear to be more irritations or even obstacles. All I can say is, as I experienced so long ago, "are you ready for your life to change completely?"

ABOUT THE AUTHOR: CONNIE VIVEROS

Connie Viveros is a Master Integrative Life Coach who helps people find more meaning in their lives and overcome the often unexplained emotional pain that keeps them from experiencing life's true joy.

Connie is professionally trained as a Master Integrative Coach through the Ford Institute for Transformation, and is certified in multiple Integrated Coaching Modules. She is also a professionally trained Certified Passion Test Facilitator and a Master Spiritual Channel and Intuitive.

Connie started her coaching business in 2008 to help other others deal with the sometimes overwhelming prospect of authentically changing their lives. If you have a desire in your heart to create lasting change in some area of your life – relationships, body image, work or career – Connie can help you unlock what has been holding you back, and transform pain into possibility to achieve just about anything you desire.

Prior to coaching, she spent many successful years as a corporate professional while devoting decades to her own spiritual growth and personal exploration. Through training and certification with the Ford Institute, Connie has discovered the embodiment of what she has sought for so long: true self love! If you are willing to create your greatest life, profound relationships, and follow your dreams then she would love to coach you to success.

Today Connie offers a wide range of programs and services - from individual coaching, to seminars and workshops, as well as keynote speeches. To contact Connie, please visit her website www.ConnieViveros.com.

Chapter 12

Expanding with Kindness & Joy
By Sylvia Puentes

What can the KINDNESS and JOY you BE create in the world? Are you ready to explore the infinite possibilities?

I wrote this chapter as an invitation to you and to the world for the expansion of a kinder, more joyful planet. Crazy you may say, and yet there is a whisper of a possibility blowing through my awareness, that now, more than ever, this can be a reality. What if your choice could inspire at least one other person to choose more kindness and joy today? And what if that alone could change the world?

This chapter is about the contribution you are that you perhaps have never acknowledged before. So if you consider yourself a catalyst, a leader or even just curious about what this may change, add and create in your life and the world than keep reading. As you read, notice what comes up for you...Does it lighten up your world, do you begin to smile? If there is, then maybe there is something here for you. What if you truly do know what is true for you?

What do you know that no one else knows?

Now when I speak about knowing I am referring to the instant awareness of something, it isn't a thought or an effort of figuring things out, you just know.

Someone once asked me, "Sylvia, what is it that you know?" Although, it appeared as a random question there was a wide open space of real curiosity, no expectation or judgment that invited me to tap into what I had never put into words before. A true gift!

As I searched for the words to describe what I had always known since a very early age I was moved to tears to finally verbalize it and have it be received.

What I know...

I know that I am kind, that I have always been kind.

I know that I am a happy joyful person and this is just a choice.

I know that when you don't judge yourself it is the greatest kindness you can gift YOU, the planet and everyone around you.

I know that life can be easy; that there is no such thing as problems, that it is all an invention.

I know that life and living can be fun, yes FUN!

This one question, "What do you know?" opened the door to so much more; it gave voice to the awareness I had been refusing. In that moment I also became aware that the question had invited me to reveal what I knew. It was as if the question, from a space of true curiosity, became the key that unlocked a future never seen before, acknowledged or spoken. Again, it was one question that unlocked the awareness. I realized that up until that point I had not been willing to be different than most of the people around me. It's as if this reality had me believe that I needed to align, agree or resist and react to everything around me in order to fit in. And when you don't, you are considered someone without reference points, someone that doesn't stand for anything, someone that doesn't belong to anything, and that, in this reality is a problem.

What is it that you know that you have been refusing to acknowledge you know, that if you were to acknowledge you know would change all realities?

What have you defined as true?

What questions would you be willing to ask to unlock what you know is true for you? Here are a few to play with. Again, remember that a question is meant to unlock your awareness, so invite you to allow yourself to go beyond what you think is the 'right answer'.

What does kindness mean to you?

_____

_____

_____

_____

What does not being kind mean to you?

_____

_____

_____

_____

When was the last time you were the energy of kindness?

_____

_____

_____

_____

What and where were you?

_____

_____

_____

What does joy mean to you?

_____

_____

_____

_____

What have you made joy mean that it isn't?

_____

_____

_____

_____

When was the last time you recall yourself being truly joyful?

_____

_____

_____

_____

What have you made kindness and joy mean that it isn't that if you were to let the definition go would allow to be all of you?

Have you turned off your kindness and joy?

Several years ago, I was in a class facilitated by Dr. Dain Heer. He asked me the question, "When was the last time you were truly happy?" I recall searching for the most recent moment, and I searched and I searched and I searched. Wow, to my surprise there had not been a recent memory that was truly an energy of being joyful. As I noticed how far I had to search for the joyful memory I was filled with sadness. I was sad that I had to go as far back as three years old to recall the innocence of playful joy. Could that be true? I actually thought I was a joyful person.

When had that changed for me? As a young girl, I recall wanting to make my father happy. Somewhere I was aware that he was requiring kindness, acknowledgement and caring. I would desperately reach out to him, especially when he was drinking. The interesting thing was, what I wasn't aware of at a young age was that he was not able to receive the huge amount of caring I had for him. Somehow the kindness I was offering was never accepted and received. Each time I would approach him to speak, hug or just sit nearby he would say "*Que quieres, barbera?*" (What do you want, kiss ass?) So what does a young girl make that mean? I made it mean that he was probably correct and I had a hidden agenda, I couldn't possibility be that kind to just wish to gift him a hug or kindness for no reason other than just a gift. I must have wanted something in return...So I thought, and bought it as true for over 30 years.

What have you made so true about you that it isn't that if you were to let it go would gift you more of you?

What does kindness and joy have to do with expansion?

What is the energy of expansion to you? For me, expansion

has a lightness to it; it's an energy, space and consciousness that that contributes to anything growing beyond the limitations we have seen as real.

Gary Douglas, the founder of Access Consciousness® talks about consciousness this way: "Consciousness and Oneness includes everything and judges nothing. It's the ability to be present in your life in every moment without judgment of you or anyone else. It's the ability to receive everything, to judge nothing, and to allow the entire Universe to be what it is."

After years of working with people of all ages around the world I discovered that the greatest threat to this reality is kindness and joy. It is a generative and creative energy that can penetrate through limitations and barriers of this reality and expand your life and living beyond what you thought was possible. Unfortunately, what we have seen or experienced on this planet is people who say they are being kind and aren't, people who are gifting and expecting something in return. So many people have concluded that KINDNESS isn't possible on this planet and that there is always a secret agenda. What if there is something else possible now?

Kindness is something that we always question and it often times what we refuse. It's all the points of view we have about if somebody is really being kind or if they are trying to create an obligation. If somebody gives you a gift, you may question if it is done from kindness or is it done from obligation? Often people give gifts from obligation, not from kindness. When you have someone who gives real kindness it "feels" different.

What if the greatest unkindness you've ever done is to judge you? Would you be willing to be the kindness towards you that you always hoped someone else would be towards you?

Whispers of Possibilities

Have you ever followed the whisper of your awareness even when it didn't make sense? What if the whispers of possibilities are of the whispers of expansion? Would you be willing to follow the light feather touch of a whisper?

I was at the grocery store the other day when I chose to buy flowers. I so enjoy adding flowers to my living space. So as I searched for what flowers wanted to come to my home there was a pink arrangement that stood out. I was surprised a bit and I almost didn't grab them because I never buy pink flowers (interesting point of view). Yet there was a whisper of an awareness...so I grabbed them and gave it no further thought. As soon as I turned the corner this young girl maybe four years old smiled ear to ear and said "flowers". There was such a joy in her world as she too perceived the magic and beauty of this bundle. So I continued to shop, got to the register to pay and on the next isle I saw the little girl again. In an instant I knew, they were meant for her.

I paid for them and walked over to her mom and asked if I may gift her daughter the flowers. It brought me so much joy to see this little girl light up in gratitude and joy to have these flowers of her very own to take home. She repeatedly said thank you and the energy of kindness and joy filled the entire grocery store (and possibly beyond that too). It added so much to my day, to one acknowledge that I followed the whisper and second to perceive what a true gift with no expectation or conclusion can create for someone else. I wonder what this choice will add and change in the world. Did this choice contribute to the energy of expansion? There was a sense of lightness and a smile on my face....and although I may never actually know what that created for the young four-year-old, I know that expanded my world. How does it get any better than that?

When you have kindness for you filled with the space of allowance, gratitude, honor, trust, and vulnerability – you then can BE and RECEIVE all of YOU. It's your permission to create you at every moment and to create your reality.

ABOUT THE AUTHOR: SYLVIA PUENTES

Sylvia Puentes has worked with children and families for over 20 years. Her experience as a mother, teacher and coach for parents and students in academia have given her a wealth of knowledge to what is actually going to create the change people seek.

As a Certified Facilitator of Access Consciousness®, Certified Life Coach, International Speaker and Teacher Trainer she contributes tools and techniques that can transform any area of life. Her work also includes courses in leadership and employees engagement for companies. Her kind presences creates a space of ease in working with individuals and groups to clear limitations and open the door to endless possibilities for a different reality.

Today she is traveling around the world sharing her vision of how empowering people to know that they know creates success in life; school, work and home. Her desire is to reach as many people as possible, in person, print, radio and television and inspire them choose to live a life with Ease, Joy & Glory.

Sylvia Puentes is an effervescent international speaker & leader in consciousness around the world. Be warned, her energy is contagious! She is a joyful and kind invitation to play with the Access Consciousness® tools to create a life and living filled with ease, joy and infinite possibilities. If you are willing to explore something different, clear limitations and choose to receive more of the GIFT YOU BE in the world than tune in and playfully turn everything that's not working for you upside down and ignite the radiant energy of YOU! **Are you ready to explore the infinite possibilities?**

You can find Sylvia here:
SylviaPuentes.AccessConsciousness.com.

Chapter 13

Living Without Limits in Your Expansive New Paradigm
By Nirmada Kaufman

What if you being you is the greatest gift the World has ever known?

The concept of YOU being the valuable product is so true and yet this reality and the old paradigm does everything it can to stop you from expanding into new and explosive possibilities. What if your relationship to yourself, to others, and to every molecule on this Earth could contribute to expanding every area of your life?

What if you just being you was enough, regardless of what other people say or choose? What if your own expansion is actually only limited by believing that other people will give it to you? Often times, in the old paradigm of relationship, if you are looking great, walking tall and strutting your stuff, the first thing people say to you is "You must be in love!" It's often assumed that you could only be that expansive and phenomenal if you're in a relationship. After several years and many failed relationships, I finally realized that this was one of the biggest lies I had bought from this reality.

After clearing multiple layers of old stuck energy and lifetimes of limiting beliefs, I finally came to realize and choose the expansion of my own life, living and reality, as an ongoing phenomenal journey. Every molecule and person on this planet can contribute to you on this magnificent journey called your life, however it's up to you to choose an expansive life and create it for yourself.

If you desire for your wildest dreams to expand into your living reality, it takes being a radical demand for yourself to be and do whatever it takes for this expansion to be realized. Ultimately, the only person that can ever stop you, is you!

One radical demand that I've always had for myself has been to not ever be stopped by anyone or anything. Sometimes we stop ourselves from committing to expanding our own life and reality by being attached to limitations created from preconceived ideas and conclusions about what we can and can't receive.

Receiving from Every Molecule in the Universe

What if you could receive from every molecule in the universe? What if every molecule in the universe is just waiting to gift to you in every moment of every day? The saying, "Ask and you shall receive" is part of what it takes to being a radical demand for yourself in the ongoing journey called the expansion of you.

One of the many things shared in this chapter that I've learned from Gary Douglas, the founder of Access Consciousness®, is to ask questions for receiving awareness. When you are welcoming awareness it expands your reality and is the ultimate in possibility. One question you can ask is, "How can I use this to my advantage?" This means that you are willing to use any experience in your life to your advantage for gaining more awareness, which opens doors to new possibilities. When you get out of judging your choices and life experiences as 'right or wrong', 'good or bad', you allow yourself to expand to a new level of freedom, joy and possibility.

What if everything the old paradigm says is true and significant is really just a lie? What if every experience and every relationship you have ever had could be a gift and a contribution to your life, living, and reality? This reality concludes that so many things are wrong and bad, and therefore we should protect ourselves by putting up barriers. When we put up barriers, what actually occurs is that this limits our capacity to receive and expand into new possibilities. What if, when things get unsteady in our life, we could just lower all of our barriers and receive everything without a point of view?

If you could wave a magic wand and have total allowance for every choice you have ever made, would you choose this? There may not be an actual magic wand for this, however the closest I've ever come to knowing this to be true is from the act of letting go of points of view – of things needing to be 'right or wrong', 'good or bad'.

Your Point of View Creates Your Reality

If your point of view creates your reality, then what points of view can you change that will change your reality? For example, if you desire more expansion in any area of your life, what points of view specifically could you change that would allow this to occur?

Asking questions is a great way to change any situation from a contractive state to an expansive space. When you ask questions such as, "What question can I ask to be more expansive?" or "What point of view can I change here to have more expansion in my life?" these are easy ways to create change in any area of your life.

Being a Radical Demand for Expansion

As previously mentioned, I've always been a radical demand for myself to not ever be stopped by anyone or anything and to never quit. I've always known since I was a young child that I came here in this life for total awareness no matter what it looks like and no matter what it takes. After being exposed to the tools of Access Consciousness® I finally came to realize that the change and expansion required for having more awareness never shows up like you imagined.

Sometimes the change and expansion shows up in really bizarre and uncomfortable ways and other times it's like a warm summer breeze gently caressing your skin. When you get out of needing to have points of view about things needing to be 'good or bad', 'right or wrong' you allow yourself the freedom of choice to expand and receive new possibilities that are beyond what you have imagined possible.

One area in life that had been less than expansive for me was in romantic relationships. I had for many years concluded that I was really bad in relationship and that it could never work for me. After finally realizing that my points of view were creating my reality and keeping me in the old paradigm of relationship, I changed my points of view and it dramatically changed my reality. Though my new paradigm of relationship doesn't look like anything I've ever imagined, it is now a living reality created from asking questions and being willing have an ongoing adventure in living.

New Paradigm of Relationship

One radical demand I made for myself was that I was going to get out of the old paradigm of relationship and start the adventure of living without limits. At the time that I made this demand, I had no idea what was going to show up next.

On a warm Costa Rican evening I met my enjoyable other in the steamy waters of the Arenal Volcanic hot springs. From the moment we met, there was an expansive level of effortless ease and joy we had together. As our relationship unfolded, we realized that one thing that contributed to it working so well, was that we had a harmony and intimacy together that neither of us had experienced before. We shared an expanded awareness together with the elements of honor, trust, vulnerability, allowance and gratitude.

I had up until this moment, always seen my expansion in the world only possible in relationship. Once I met my enjoyable other, everything changed. It was the first time in my life that having a romantic relationship was about me fully being me and the other person fully being themselves. From the moment that we met, and up until this day we have been partners in consciousness and expand each other's realities by being ourselves.

We never ask the other person to be anything other than who they are and support one another to expand into new possibilities daily. Asking each other questions for creating change and expansion is a part of our daily rituals. Whenever anything gets strange in either of our lives, we ask questions for changing the energy from a contraction to an expansion.

One of our favorite 'go to questions' to ask the other when either of us gets contracted, is, "Are you being you right now?". Every time we have asked this question of each other the reply is always, "No!". When you realize you are not being you, it becomes easier for you to change the energy into a more expansive and joyful possibility.

We practice our intimacy with each other on a daily basis. Though we naturally have a level of intimacy with each other, we also desire to expand into being more both as individuals as well as partners in consciousness.

When we honor each other, it's about honoring the other person's choices even if it's not what we would choose. We practice honoring where the other person is at regardless of what we ourselves are choosing. This has been an ongoing journey of practicing to continually honor each other and our choices, and requires functioning from creating a relationship beyond judgment. There is really nothing greater or more nurturing than being seen by someone from the eyes of no judgment.

We trust that the other person is going to be and do what the other person is going to be and do. In the rare moments when either of us has had a point of view that didn't support this trust, it created a contraction. Once we became aware of this, we asked questions to clear the limiting points of view and this created a new level of expansion and awareness.

Vulnerability is something that we came together having in communion from the first moment onwards. There are no barriers up to one another and this allows for so much awareness and expansion to be contributed to one another. It's also really different from what we've seen being done in relationship out in the world and it creates an energy that changes everyone around us. We truly have so much fun being partners in consciousness together as there is no 'right or wrong' way that we are allowed to be playmates together. We just keep choosing what's fun for us and what works for us, moment by moment.

We practice having and expanding allowance for ourselves and each other on a daily basis. As our partnership in consciousness expands, so does our level of awareness. As our awareness grows, it becomes essential for our allowance to also grow. One thing we have learned over time, is that if the other person is having an upset, and we ourselves have allowance for the situation without a point of view of it being 'good or bad', 'right or wrong', this creates the space for the other person to change and expand. There is an ease and harmony created in every area of life and relationship by practicing expanding allowance.

Gratitude is one of the greatest gifts I've ever known or experienced in my life. It rapidly expands and changes any situation into something greater. In my relationship with my enjoyable other, it has been a tool that we play with daily. When we are having fun we use it to create more fun. And on the occasional moments that we are having an argument, it always changes and expands the energy. Rather than either one of us continuing to fight for the rightness of our points of view, we pause and express three things we are grateful for about each other. This always creates new level of freedom and expansion both for ourselves and for our relationship.

The New Paradigm of You Being You

Being YOU is truly the greatest gift the world has ever known!

If you were truly being you, who would you be?

If you were truly being you, where would you be?

If you were truly being you, when would you be?

If you were truly being you, how would you be?

Are you willing to be daring and to find out?

Welcome to your new expansive paradigm in the adventure of living!

What else is possible now that you have never considered before?

ABOUT THE AUTHOR: NIRMADA KAUFMAN

Nirmada, *The Radical Demand Diva*, is an author, pragmatic futurist and an Access Consciousness®Facilitator. She is best known for empowering and facilitating the seekers around the world who are demanding change and are ready for it now.

With a radically effective and pragmatic approach she guides seekers to be a radical demand for themselves so they create the life and future they really desire. Nirmada is the co-author of the book *Love in the Next 10 Seconds, Changing the Box of Relationship into Living Without Limits.*

Chapter 14

Expanding Beyond Limitations

By Minette the Internal Energist

H ello beautiful! Chances are if you are reading this, you are looking for change in this reality and your own life. I'm so honored and grateful that you chose and that you are choosing to look for ways to shift or change your reality. What if you choosing to expand your energy is all that is required for this change to happen?

The energy of expansion...what does that mean to you? To me it means expanding beyond any and all limitations that you may have created for yourself in any time or space. Expanding can be scary, exhilarating, and exciting but without expansion we cannot hope to change our circumstances and start making bigger choices in our lives. There are many different circumstances or points in our life that we can choose to expand and create change or we can contract from and limit our potential for creation in that situation. When we choose to create and have something different we are choosing from the space of awareness. It's this awareness that is a catalyst for change, it makes us aware that we have a choice in everything that happens in our life. Our choice is whether we and contract or expand our energy into it.

I want to talk to you more about energy because once we begin to understand that everything is energy, our whole world can change, but first:

Let me tell you the story of how my whole world changed and how my journey began to becoming Minette the Internal Energist. It was a time in my life when I could have contracted but instead chose to expand my energy.

My life was what some might call perfect; husband, two kids, good job, nice house. Then one day I slipped, fell, hit my head and lost consciousness. X-rays were taken and I was informed I was going to be OK. Over the course of the following year, I developed problems with my liver, gallbladder, and thyroid. It was as if my body was shutting down (and it was). I had limited use of my left hand, excruciating pain and headaches. This left me unable to perform the duties of my job. I ended up having to leave my job and within six months of me leaving, my husband was laid off. We then had no income and two children to support. Being unable to pay our bills, the bank was starting to foreclose on our home. We were going to lose everything. "How can it get any worse?" I was thinking. But it did, my pain kept getting worse, nothing was working, so then I got an appointment with a specialist who ordered an MRI and informed me my neck was broken. I needed surgery immediately! I cried and could not believe this was happening. I had the surgery and the days after surgery were horrible, I felt immense pain and was very worried. I was terrified, not only for my health and recovery, but for my family's future; where our family would live, how would we survive. When I was at my lowest point, I asked, "what was next?".

The future seemed dismal (mind you, I have never considered myself a victim throughout my lifetime. I have always considered myself a survivor who could handle anything, such as my childhood, which is a whole different story.). So I made a demand, "No more feeling sorry for yourself, Minette". I thought about all the people in the world who had it tougher than me and who were truly grateful for what little they had. There were stories of people who overcame hardship by choosing something different, so I chose to have something different as well. I choose to have gratitude for everything, to expand into the energy of gratitude, and with this choice my whole life changed. I had gratitude for the beautiful home I lived in, for however long I got to live there. I was grateful for my health and the fact that I could still walk, for my family, who I loved so very much and who were helping to take care of me so wonderfully during my recovery. I began to wake every morning saying to myself, "I am grateful for every breath, every step, every heartbeat," and with this energy of gratitude that I was embracing and surrounding myself with, changes came almost immediately. My recovery hastened, my pain lessened, our finances improved, we got to keep our home. How does it get any better than that!?! And it keeps getting better. I have a successful business doing what I LOVE; working with people to create greater possibilities in their life.

Now back to energy, this rapid shift in my reality sparked a curiosity in me to discover more about energy and how we create and choose to react to our circumstances. Could it be as simple as choice and the energy that my thoughts of gratitude created?

So I began my research. I had always been fascinated by the sciences of biology, physics and psychology, but then I realized that all of these have a connection and the connection was energy. Without energy there would be no life, there would be no movement, no sound, no feelings, no emotions, no color and definitely no us!! Everything is energy and all energy has a vibration and frequency. Every emotion, every thought, every feeling we have creates a different vibrational frequency. WOW, this blew my mind. I learned that my frequency can affect your frequency and yours can affect mine.

Have you ever felt someone enter the room and felt that person's energy so strong you noticed that every person in the room felt their energy too? It draws people in and makes them want to be friends with them or be near them. It's because their energy was vibrating at such a high frequency it was as if everyone in the room was drawn to them and the same is true for low frequencies. Have you ever entered a room and felt a heaviness or had someone start to talk and you could instantly feel your energy shift. That is us responding to other people's frequencies and energy.

So now that we know that everything is energy and all energies have a different frequency, let's get into some of these frequencies. There are high frequencies such as love, gratitude, joy, peace, enthusiasm, serenity, cheerfulness etc. Then there are low frequencies; insecurity, blame, worry, fear, anger, jealousy, regret, etc. Each of these emotions or thoughts creates a different energy in the body, with its own different frequency. These frequencies not only affect our emotional well being, they affect our physical health as well. So when we surround ourselves with lower frequencies our mind and body suffers. Now know this, we do not attract what we want, we attract what we put our energy into. Have you ever heard of the law of attraction? We attract what we think about, we attract like frequencies. Our cells are very intelligent and respond to all frequencies around us, the thoughts we have, the movies we watch, the music we listen to and the people we surround ourselves with, so choose wisely. Now how can we use this knowledge to start creating our new reality filled with what we choose?

Start with loving yourself, if we tell ourselves every day, I am so tired, I am so sick, I hate my body etc, what affect do you think these energies and frequencies have on your body? Be kind to yourself. You are the only YOU in this whole world. Do you realize what a phenomenal, precious gift you are? No one else has your exact talents, skills, thoughts, capacities or energy frequency. Appreciate the amazing gift you are. From this energy and space of self love, there are infinite possibilities for creating.

Know what it is you want to create in your life. Is it happiness, abundance, joy? Whatever it is imagine it, feel it, start each day with the energy of this feeling. This is your target and holding this energy and frequency will attract things that will contribute to this change. Keep an open mind with no expectations of how these changes could show up. (This one makes me chuckle because before my accident I wondered every day, "how I could have more time to spend with my family?" Now I am a lot more conscious of all my thoughts and wishes).

Be aware throughout the day when you find yourself in a situation where you would normally contract and go into judgment of yourself or someone else, stop and take a moment to envision the path you are about to choose. Will you choose the lower frequency of judgment, blame, fear etc, or the other path, the higher frequency of allowance, peace, joy, happiness? Now choose the path that will create more of what you want in your life. Also, know that this new energy you are choosing may make some people uncomfortable (usually, these people are choosing a low frequency life). Not everyone is going to choose to be surrounded by these higher frequencies. Maintain a space of allowance, allow others to choose their path without judgment, having no judgment is very important, whether they choose low or high frequencies. It is not up to us, our only responsibility is to our self. Only we have the power to make ourselves happy, so your choice is who or what you allow into your space. I've found that some of these people who were choosing the lower frequencies were unaware they had a choice and that there was another possibility. My higher vibrations raised their awareness and they started making different choices. Also some of these people in my life that were once uncomfortable and repelled by my higher frequency had started to come around again, curious of what I was doing different and noticing the immense change I had created in my life. So know you choosing to function from this higher frequency will be an invitation to some, for a life of greater possibilities.

Being an invitation to greater possibilities is very exciting. There can also be times when it can be a little scary because you are choosing something new and creating from a space you have not known before (this is necessary for change, I mean if everything was so great before why would you be looking for change). If you ever find yourself stuck, just ask, "what can I choose that would create more?" and do not look for an answer, asking the question is what will shift your vibrational frequency into one that creates more possibilities rather than staying stuck and limiting your possibilities. You will find that when you start to function from the space of choice and surround yourself by higher frequencies, you will have a greater possibility for creating the life you have always desired.

Things to remember:

1. Know what it is you want to create.

Wake in the morning with the energy of these creations.

2. Be aware when you are around someone or something with lower frequencies.

Limit exposure to these people or situations as much as possible.

3. Make choices that will create more in your life.

Instead of contracting, choose the energy of expansion for creation.

4. Even choosing not to make a choice is a choice.

No one can make you happy except yourself, so don't wait for another to choose it for you.

5. LOVE YOURSELF!!

When we raise our vibration, this is an invitation for others to participate, they are drawn to you and the energy of your beautiful frequency.

Much gratitude for you and the contribution you are. How much change can we create in this reality with our energy of expansion?

ABOUT THE AUTHOR: MINETTE THE INTERNAL ENERGIST

My name is Minette Sanchez, also known as the Internal Energist. I am a certified professional life coach, Energy Worker, Access Consciousness® Certified Bars Practitioner and Facilitator, as well as an Access Consciousness® Certified Body Process Facilitator, radio show host, motivational speaker, and author, with a background in business and psychology. I am the proud owner of Internal Energies, a company whose goal is to help people create more ease, joy, and possibilities in all aspects of their life (relationships, finances, body).

I was born in California and have been blessed with an amazing husband, Eric, who I have had the joy and pleasure of creating the last 25 years of my life with, and looking forward to many more. We have two sweet, kind, highly intelligent and beautiful daughters; Ashlyn and Jocelyn. I am filled with gratitude and so much love for my AMAZING family, whose love and support has allowed me to go on this beautiful journey. I am also so grateful and filled with joy for this amazing life I am living, and enjoy everyday getting to share that joy with my clients and helping them create more happiness and possibilities in their lives as well.

As an Internal Energist, I get to assist people daily in creating and finding ways to enjoy more ease with their bodies, I am trained to perform and teach over 50 different energetic body processes as well as coaching clients to achieve more of what they desire in their life with family, children, work, finances and so much more. So, if you are ready to create more joy and ease in your life or body, visit www.internalenergies.com.

Chapter 15

The Key to Your Secret Mind

By Cherie Lawrence

C an I invite you into an unfamiliar world inside your head? A secret place, hidden within your mind...the key holder? I know you are wondering, how could such a place exist? You may not even be able to believe this, but the key holder (my subconscious mind), held safely out of my reach the memory of a non-corporeal being borrowing my body. The audacity!

I will explain de-compartmentalization and how it will help you spontaneously expand your energy and awareness. I will give you tools that you can use to recover the magical experiences tucked away in *your* mind. And if my experience is any indication, they are experiences that could answer the questions you've long had about the universe.

You may already know about the subconscious mind being a place in your mind that stores information that isn't readily available to you. In the self-help field we believe that the subconscious mind stores a lot of information that can hold you back. When your mind holds information from you, it isn't trying to deceive you, it is doing this to protect you.

If you've had an experience outside of your comfort zone, outside the realm of what you've learned should be possible, then your mind may be protecting you from the "discomfort" of conflicting values. Which is fine... but, what if you've had an experience that answers the biggest question you have about the universe. What if you've had an experience that, if you remembered it, it would bring you great joy? What if locked inside your head is proof that a life of magic and possibilities are real?

Want to find out? Me too!

We all have superpowers (did you know?) and mine is being an energy virtuoso. Right now I'll create the space for you to have a more complete awareness. You may even start remembering things you can't believe you've forgotten – immediately! Like me.

We often think we have to "do" something to make something happen, but just "being" can be far more productive. For example, you being with me right now can lead to spontaneous expansion." In fact this can be called "an Activation!"

So let me ask you, are you willing to go beyond your perception, beyond the bounds of what we've learned is being "human," beyond the confines of this reality? Are you willing to walk into the unknown of your secret desires for an impossible life? What do you secretly wish was true about life and living that maybe *is* true about life and living? Would you be willing to expand and find out how magical life can be?

Expansion is the magic and it happens when you are willing to see that there is much more to life than you currently know, perceive, and experience. But sometimes there are reasons why you might feel unwilling or blocked.

The biggest reason for leaving the unexplored, unexplored in any area is fear. The two biggest fears tend to be: 1) Fear of what others would say or think if they knew what you are doing or thinking and 2) You seeing and realizing how powerful and potent you are. When you expand, you go into the unexplored, despite the limitations you have previously imposed upon yourself and those imposed upon you by others. Is now the time for your expansion?

Our subconscious mind has a default setting – "comfortable." That's how it works, because it thinks that "comfortable" equals "safe." So if we experience something that is in direct conflict with our current beliefs - something that could make us feel really uncomfortable and confused – the mind will protect us from that information by making us forget it even happened. Because otherwise, how would we process that experience? The subconscious mind quickly resets us back to "comfort." This is true even if being completely stressed out 24 hours a day is comfortable to us because it is familiar, so our mind will keep that as our experience in our reality.

So anything you may have experienced – anything that was completely out of touch with this reality and beyond your comfort zone, and in direct conflict with the opinions of people you care about, well you may have forgotten about it. And I mean entire experiences, not just thoughts or ideas, but actual events, *'poof'* gone from your mind, memories completely out of your reach, swallowed by a black hole.

If this sounds unbelievable, that too is the handy work of your subconscious mind. It's protected you well from the discomfort so you have no frame of reference for such an experience existing in the first place. Anything connected to or that could lead you to a forgotten experience, would also be forgotten. You would think that you'd know if you had some out of this reality experience right? Or would you?

The thing is, if your mind has compartmentalized the experience, you wouldn't remember. Let me explain compartmentalization.

Compartmentalization is your innate ability to separate events, experiences, or thoughts that are in direct conflict with values, cognitions, emotions, beliefs, etc. within yourself. This includes entire events. This prevents any cognitive dissonance, or the mental discomfort and anxiety that the event, experience, or thought may have caused.

All of this information may be making it feel a little like your world is spinning or being turned upside down, especially if you haven't been delving into subjects that are "out there" "questionable" or push the envelope of your reality – and that's okay. But let's wonder together – How much fun and ease you can have exploring this? I'd like to say that anything that may come up for you in this chapter is something that will most expeditiously move your life forward to the life you truly desire. Simply by reading and being with the pages of this chapter, you will be participating in an activation for you and your magical life – an activation that will propel your life into that which you truly desire to experience, but haven't previously had the awareness or willingness to explore before.

One of my targets in life has been to go beyond, you know like Star Trek, "where no one has gone before." And even with that as my target, I know that I have compartmentalized experiences I'd love to have conscious awareness of. That's why I've been inviting and allowing de-compartmentalization for areas of interest to me. As an energy virtuoso, when I share my stories, I know that they will activate something in you too, allowing you to access expansive possibilities within yourself.

What follows are two of my de-compartmentalized experiences. As you read them, you may feel emotional. You may cry, you may feel anger, you may feel happiness, you may feel joy, you may remember something. You may want to know more about me, you may immediately dislike me. The possibilities are endless! No matter what you feel while reading about my experiences, something will change within you. Being connected to my raw, real, open experiences can send a ripple through your entire being, if you're willing to receive it, if it's time for you.

Your own life will begin to change and if you allow it, de-compartmentalization will occur. Of course your experiences won't necessarily be the same as mine. Your stories could be completely different, or on different subjects all together.

I've added a very specific frequency and energy to these words. As you read them they are activating you at the deepest level, and if you'll receive it, they are unrolling the red carpet of magic and possibilities that you've secretly or not so secretly desired.

Activation 1:

When I was 11 years old I was adopted and the home was completely dysfunctional. The environment created by the parental figures was so mean and brutal that if I was aware of the concept of suicide, I probably would have chosen it. If someone even hinted that I could end my life as a possibility, I think I would have.

The home itself was actually a beautiful home in the woods. It was surrounded by beauty, there was a stream and hills

I loved to climb. It was only when I was in the house that I cried out to God asking what I had done to deserve such a life. I spent my nights crying myself to sleep asking God to take me from there.

I was a very aware child, I knew what people were feeling, I knew when someone didn't like me, I knew when they hated me, but I had no frame of reference for where those feelings originated from. Naturally I blamed myself.

I used to have recurring dreams of a space ship hovering above our home in the woods. It was always night time, the ship was silver, there was a blue light at the base of it, it was saucer-like, it spun slowly as it hovered above. I knew it was there and I was terrified. I knew they were there for me. A blue light would shine down upon the house and I would disappear from my bed.

I always remembered myself going through some sort of pinball machine, with me being the ball. My body turned into a ball of energy. While I didn't see the structure of the pinball, it felt that way because of all the different "turns" before reaching the destination.

The next thing I remember is popping out of what seemed like the machine to having my whole body back. I was next sitting on a throne and there are extraterrestrial (in this case Highly Evolved Beings) beings around me. I was very afraid, terrified of what was happening. But I remember the beings having grey faces, rather large heads, almond-shaped eyes and being very kind. They spoke to me in my mind trying to reassure me that I was safe. I told them I wanted to go home, I just wanted to go home.

They began telling me that they came for me and that I was a queen in this galaxy or planet. I didn't want to understand what they were saying, nor did I care about what they were saying. I just cried that I wanted to go home. They tried to calm me and I just tried to escape. I kicked and screamed. They eventually sent me back to my bed.

Now, I kept this experience as a recurring dream for years until I totally forgot about the dream. Since my invitation of de-compartmentalization I've come to remember it in greater detail and greater understanding.

The event wasn't a dream, it really happened. Extraterrestrial beings came to me in a time of great need to give me some respite from my intense emotional pain. It was a recurring dream because they took me several times in trying to help me remember who I was and to envelope me in the higher energy of their higher evolved environment. What I experienced as the pinball was my mind's interpretation of the experience of my body moving into a different dimensionality.

I've always had team mates who've been at my side. I've always been taken care of and I always will be taken care of. So, how could I have forgotten such experiences? Well in my defense, they made me forget that the experience was "real" because it was something I decided was traumatic, so they didn't want to add that stress to my conscious life experience which was already traumatic. They wanted me to have a sense of them in my awareness so they left it in my mind as a dream, the way I could most easily receive them.

Then I'd even forgotten about this entire thing, even as a dream for a while. Highly Evolved beings, extraterrestrials, aliens aren't real. That's the official standpoint of the U.S. government, even though more and more respected high ranking officials are coming forward with personal accounts and stories of their experiences to the contrary.

Even as I'm writing this, I'm remembering and understanding more and more. It's like a point specific key is opening my mind. And like a key, me and my experiences are unlocking you, is it your time? Are you willing to have it?

Activation 2:

Now this is an experience I seriously can't believe I had forgotten. I've told you that one of my targets is to go where no one has gone before and essentially to go beyond the confines of this reality and find out what the possibilities are, even beyond my imagination. So when I experience a fear in a subject of interest to me, my reflex is to move into it even further.

The shower is a place of great peace, cleansing, and the easiest place for expansion I've found inside my home. Water seems to be a conduit of space and expansion.

One day I was in the shower, talking to the Universe about my life, and asking what contribution I can be to the world, doing my usual thing. Suddenly I felt a very distinct energy presence. I don't mean like a disembodied entity, it felt far larger, faster vibrating, like I could touch it. I immediately knew something big was going to happen. I knew that I needed to relax my body to the greatest degree possible. I was both afraid and excited. I started taking deep breaths to move into my higher mind and beyond my conscious mind. My curiosity was beyond peaked, I breathed, I was nervous.

The next thing I knew, there was a separate other being in my mind, I felt the rumbling like a vibrational earthquake inside my head, but it wasn't scary. The being in my mind felt so calm, still, and peaceful. She said that she was me, a future me, and she wanted to know what it's like to be in a body. I felt fear come up immediately, and questions. How on earth would that happen? I simply said yes and there was an intense surge within my body, I took some deep hard breaths and suddenly I'm in the back seat of my mind. We're both in my head, but I'm in the back and aware of everything. I'm just not in control of anything. And I didn't try to take control of anything.

The first thing she did was experience each and every drop of water on her arms, almost as if it was in slow motion. She had total presence. She was totally and completely present. I was experiencing what it's like to be in the absolute NOW moment, which for me is the ELUSIVE NOW. Each drop of water that hit her body was like first time. It felt like a good sensation that went through her body in waves. She experienced it and did something I would totally not do. She got my hair wet and ran her fingers through my hair. I wouldn't get my hair wet until I was actually ready to separately wash my hair. She examined my body. She looked at and felt each and every inch of it. She was especially drawn to the female parts, my breasts and vagina. It was total exploration and continuous moments of the first time.

Then she did something I totally didn't expect. She called for my husband from the shower. The way she spoke, it was, how do I describe it? The way she spoke was so detached, speaking in the third person. She spoke of my body as being a "vessel" and she referenced the "planet earth" and used the word "human".

She explained to him that she was exploring with my body. He was totally fine with it. He later explained that everything about me was different. Not only the way I talked, the way I moved, but my energy was totally different. He said she had a large presence, "collective, otherworldly, calm, peaceful, and curious." Yes she was very curious.

She then wanted to know if he could come into the shower, I was okay with it and my husband agreed. He came into the shower and she wrapped her arms around him. She was still completely in the now moment, taking in the sensation wet skin to skin contact.

Soon I had my body back. The whole experience lasted about an hour and was confined to the shower. I spent about a week questioning whether or not I was crazy, whether or not I made it up, whether or not it was real. My husband said it was real. It's one thing to talk differently, move differently, and act differently, but I couldn't have brought forth the presence and energy that she exuded. She had an overwhelming sense of peace and stillness that radiated outwardly.

And then at some point, I completely forgot about that experience. Wow, how?

Compartmentalization. I guess my mind decided it was too 'out there' and didn't fit in with what I've learned, so *poof* it went. Into the "black hole". I've only remembered it since inviting de-compartmentalization.

Do you feel excited, thrilled, triggered? What are you feeling inside of your body after reading this? Am I crazy? Am I a liar? Am I awesome? Are you?

Despite the fact that your compartmentalizations might be totally different in nature, it could be time for you to de-compartmentalize and come into wholeness of mind, body, and spirit. If you just felt a wave of fear, that's okay. Expanding is feeling that fear and saying yes anyway. Is it time?

Interestingly, as I was writing this, I felt an intense surge of energy which I "moved into" and there was a message from that very being! I hadn't previously heard about her experience, or communicated with her ever again. I edited the message so it's not in the third person, the way she spoke before as she didn't take over my body, she was in my mind with me as she was in the very beginning of the last experience.

"I am Rana. I am the being that has borrowed the body. My experience on earth was phenomenal. She was a fine host, my past self, she is very brave. It was so wonderful to walk with feet. I didn't realize how heavy bodies are. Gravity is quite interesting. When we (higher evolved beings) create bodies we are not subject to gravity. We are still light with our bodies. I would say that the experience of true gravity was the most unexpected thing for me. Experiencing skin to skin contact was a quite enjoyable experience. Again I felt cumbersome using heavy body due to gravity so again that was something I wasn't expecting, but it was still enjoyable. I keep coming back to gravity, I have so much respect for your bodies and your abilities to do the things that you are able to in such a high gravity environment. I wasn't able to stay as long as I desired because of the gravity."

Now this message is something I could compartmentalize. But I'm choosing not to!

I can feel that you may be raring to begin the process of de-compartmentalization and I've brought some of my favorite tools. Questions. I have some questions here for you to ask yourself for ease of de-compartmentalization. It will begin the beautiful process of de-compartmentalization if you're ready, and if you're ready, it will unlock everything required to shift into a whole new expanded reality of you. What are the infinite possibilities?

Ask the questions out loud, but don't try to answer them. Each question will bring and shift energy. After asking, take a deep breath in through your nose and release the energy out through your mouth. Asking is using your free will to co-create with the universe. Asking the questions out loud allows possibilities beyond your finite mind to show up for you. So just ask and let it go.

Ask these questions as often as you desire. Certain questions might stand out and you might ask those questions more often than the others. For more structure, I'd say ask these questions every day for the next 30 days and be aware of your experiences and forgotten memories.

You can take it a step further and keep a journal for your forgotten memories AND new experiences beyond this reality.

12 Questions to de-compartmentalization

1. Am I willing to de-compartmentalize in the areas of life, living and reality that would be a contribution to me beyond my imagination?

a) If no, am I willing to consider allowing de-compartmentalization in the areas of life, living and reality that would be a contribution to me beyond my imagination?

b) If no, what would it take for me to be willing to consider allowing de-compartmentalization in the areas of life, living and reality that would be a contribution to me beyond my imagination?

2. What de-compartmentalization could I allow and invite right now that would give me more of what I've been secretly asking for and desiring?

3. What gift and contribution can de-compartmentalization be to me?

4. How much ease can I have with de-compartmentalizing?

5. What's possible for me now that I never considered as possible before?

6. What space of de-compartmentalization could I be that if I were totally being it, would allow for all of this reality to de-compartmentalize with ease?

7. What would it take for total de-compartmentalization to occur automatically at a pace that is filled with ease and fun for me?

8. What would it take for me to feel safe and loved enough to invite de-compartmentalization into my life?

9. What question can I ask that would shift any resistance to de-compartmentalization?

10. What am I pretending not to know that I know about de-compartmentalization that if I acknowledged that I know it, would allow me to expand exponentially?

11. What am I not willing to be aware of, that if I were aware of it, would change everything?

12. What could I de-compartmentalize that would most expeditiously lead me to the life I truly desire?

Three Questions about de-compartmentalizing around Highly Evolved Beings

What gift and contribution have highly evolved beings been to me that I'm not willing to acknowledge that if I were willing to acknowledge would change everything?

What space of de-compartmentalization about highly evolved beings could I be that if I were totally being it, would allow for total de-compartmentalization with case?

What gift and contribution are highly evolved beings being to me right now that I'm not acknowledging?

I think it's important to note, in this chapter I am not referring to traumatic experiences that may have been compartmentalized as a coping mechanism. I have those too. I'm talking about the mind-blowing experiences that actually blew our minds and seemingly exploded out of existence. But if some traumatic (if you have any) experiences that have been compartmentalized are ready to be released with ease for the life you'd actually like to experience, if you are willing and ready to release that which is ready to be released from you, say yes and I wonder what ease you can have with it?

With all this being said, I'm ready for expansion to creep into the widest and deepest depths of fear which are hiding my greatness. Whoosh! Are you ready too?

Expansion is when you are confused, you don't understand, and you are scared but you still say yes. Whoosh! Expansion is going into the unknown despite your fear.

Expansion is a willingness to go beyond your perception, beyond the bounds of what we've learned is being "human", beyond the confines of this reality. Expansion is walking ever forward into the unknown of your secret desires to live an impossible life. What do you secretly wish was true about life and living that maybe *is* true about life and living? Would you be willing to expand and find out how magical life can be?

Expansion is being willing to see that there is much more to life than you currently know, perceive, and experience. What if the life you wished was real, but this reality says is science fiction, or isn't possible, really is possible? Would you be willing to have it? What if de-compartmentalization was a key to unlocking what you know about what's really possible?

Is now the time?

ABOUT THE AUTHOR: CHERIE LAWRENCE

Cherie Lawrence is an energy virtuoso who shifts realities, and creates instant change in people's lives. Having spent over 1,500 hours in personal development and self-transformation she has experience in a wide range of topics such as healing, consciousness, expansion, whole awareness, higher evolved beings and human potential. The main focus of her research at this time is creating wealth beyond one's imagination.

Find Cherie on her website at www.RealYouNow.com.

Chapter 16

The Soul Wants to Grow
By Deborah Perdue

"I am so thankful for opening my heart wider and wider – for stretching my spiritual wings. For loving myself more and more so I can love others exponentially. I am grateful for understanding and illumination and more wisdom. I am open to expansion in my life!" ~ Deborah Perdue

Expansion, the opening up of one's horizons for a greater purpose, came most dramatically in my life when my marriage of 24 years disintegrated. I remember how difficult it felt to decide to end it. Both of us struggled, and we weren't sure whether or not we were making the right decision. We had been best friends, which was a good thing, but we were also in a codependent relationship. He was a rock and roll musician, with the lifestyle that naturally accompanies that profession, and when we finally got sober in our 40s, it became sadly apparent that there was not a lot of common ground between us. At some point during that challenging and painful period, I remember hearing the phrase, "The Soul wants to grow" and now, 15 years later, I realize how absolutely true that phrase is. I'm not sure if expansion in one's life often comes from devastation and loss, but I know that in my own life, I was propelled into change through the dissolution of my marriage.

So, there I was, in my mid-40s, single for the first time in my life, feeling despair and uncertainty about my future. But despite the natural grieving I was going through, it was also exciting to look for a new area in which to live, to have my own bank account, develop new, nurturing friendships, and find my place in the world. It was, perhaps, the first time in my life that I felt so free. Like most of us, I certainly didn't feel free before leaving the nest, and I felt even less freedom given the controlling aspects of my marriage. My life was a blank, beautiful white easel and what I painted on it, and the colors I chose, was now up to me.

During the year or so of emotional struggle and uncertainty before the divorce was finalized, a number of friends in unrelated moments, suggested I visit the nearby Center for Spiritual Living in Santa Rosa, California. Not being a church-goer, I thanked each one and then tried my best to ignore them. I say "tried my best" because although I was leaving behind many negatives that created deep sadness within, and was excited to begin my new journey, I was also experiencing what we have come to refer to as a dark night of the soul. And for me, that night became so dark that after several months of trying my best to ignore the suggestion, I finally agreed to go.

The Centers for Spiritual Living are filled with people who are very open, warm, loving, and accepting. They are on a spiritual path that includes honoring all religions, and the teachings resonated deeply in my soul – a soul that wanted to grow. I got tears in my eyes the first Sunday I stepped through the doors, feeling so deeply in my heart and soul that I was among my tribe, that the things I felt within my own heart were being verbalized by the minister and that I was HOME! So, I started attending the weekly services, and in Autumn of 2001, took the beginning spiritual class offered called Foundations.

From there, the horizons of my life started expanding. I look back now and see how brave and courageous I was! My confidence had grown, I was blessed with many new friends and even started a new relationship with a wonderful man who later became my second husband. When he invited me to move to Southern Oregon with him, I didn't hesitate. With my cockatiels happily swinging in their cage in the back seat, along with our two dogs, we meandered up to Oregon, where we found a home on 5 acres, with trees and rivers and mountains as the backdrop. I have always been a country girl and it felt, and still feels, like heaven on earth.

Before I moved, I made sure there was a nearby Center for Spiritual Living. The one in Oregon became my spiritual base again, and I began eagerly taking more classes, being transformed by (actually remembering) the Truth of who I am – a part of the Divinity of God; a spiritual being having a human experience. I began to know and understand myself much better and to love myself fully. I got clear on cause and effect, knowing we are not victims, but co-creators in our lives. I gained much more compassion for others.

After six years of training, I became licensed as a practitioner for the Centers for Spiritual Living. I now teach the same classes that helped me so much. I counsel people who come to me, in a spiritually based way. It is my greatest joy to watch another person grasp the concepts for him or herself – that as co-creators we can choose again each new day. To watch someone else have an "aha" moment and then choose differently, to see someone expanding the good in his or her life, to witness another phoenix rising from the ashes, is SO gratifying to me.

Seven years ago, a minister gave the congregation blank notebooks and asked us to write five things we were grateful for, each day for 40 days, and then to watch and feel how appreciation and thankfulness would bring about more joy and peace in our lives. Ever the good student, I wrote in mine dutifully, and have continued the practice even to this day. The idea came to me to create and publish a beautiful Gratitude Journal, so others in the world could use it to find out the power of embracing gratitude.

My artist friend and soul-sister, Tara Thelen, was willing to create her gorgeous watercolor illustrations for the Journal. I included some of my most potent thoughts of thanksgiving compiled through the years, designed it, with blank pages for the readers to write in their own lists of things they felt gratitude for. We pitched it to a few publishing companies, such as Hay House, and were politely turned down. We saw little activity with The Journal for a few years, and then a couple of friends saw it and believed in it, and in us, and provided a loan for half the cost to have it printed, so we could sell it in nationally, and with this help we got it done!

Since its first printing in 2012, people have come to me with tears in their eyes, expressing how much this process of journaling has meant to them and how the practice of being thankful has resulted in a shift that has changed their lives. A young woman from the Peace Corps scanned and posted filled-out pages from her Journal in her blog, expressing deep gratitude to Tara and me for the creation of the *Grace of Gratitude Journal*, showing visually how her own grateful thoughts helped her through sadness and loneliness being away from home in a foreign country. Another young woman shared similarly that her mother gifted her the Journal and echoed how much it helped her when she moved to Alaska with her new husband. These heartfelt demonstrations mean so much to me and have added to my own list of things to be grateful for.

Through the years, I have expanded my life further in ways I never thought possible. I was extremely shy when younger, and have found my voice and confidence through my spiritual path. I have a blog, and have published articles in local print newspapers and online, on the topic of gratitude, peace and joy. Last year, I expanded my calling further by offering a four day Grace of Gratitude Retreat near Mt. Shasta with my yogi sister. The retreat was full and perfect in every way. Participants said they loved it, and so did I. I continue to teach spiritual classes such as Divine Appreciation and Self-Mastery. I now offer Daily Thoughts of Thanksgiving on the www.graceofgratitude.com website and even stretched out of my comfort zone to travel to teach Gratitude Workshops which have been well-received. Next year promises even more expansion, and while I am not sure of all the particulars yet, I am ready!

I am amazed by all that has transpired since I began opening up to life in a more expansive way. For 25 years of my adult life, I lacked self-esteem, felt unworthy and numbed myself with alcohol and drugs. The first part of my adult life was hedonistic and selfish. Now I am so content to be a catalyst and an example to others, as I help them break the chains of limitation in their own lives.

As I have thought about my own story of expansion, I realized that it comes down to seven steps which I share below. I must admit that the first phase of the expansion of my life as I divorced and set out to create a new start, was not as organized as this list below. But in the subsequent expansions detailed in this chapter, I have used these steps consciously.

Expansion of one's life is not always easy. Sometimes we resist the call to grow and expand and transform, but I truly believe that our souls DO want to grow. Had I not left my comfortable, yet stifling, lifestyle in 1999, I would not be presented with opportunities to expand. I am so grateful that I have stepped out of fear of change and let my life explode into transformation!

7 Steps to Expansion and Growth

1. Listen and tune into the guidance from within for direction, through meditation and contemplation.

Through stillness, we can gain information to help us in our journey. It probably won't be an audible voice (though it could be), but listen and wait for direction from your Higher Self. When it is time to expand and grow emotionally, spiritually, professionally or even materially, your inner self will know and start nudging you in that direction if you pay attention. It is so important to stop "doing" to give Spirit the space to inform you. Be still and know.

2. State your new intention and then feel the vibration of expansion

When we are ready to make any change or expansion in our lives, it's essential to let ourselves feel in advance the emotions we would have in the new place. Start by writing what your intention is. It could be to do work in your life that is more meaningful to you. It could be to step out and begin writing or creating artwork if you have always wanted to do that. It could be as simple as making more friends, sharing your expertise with others, having children or anything else you desire. Whatever it is for you, write down or journal what your new intention to expand is. Then spend time each day, feeling in your heart and soul how it will feel to be doing what you intend. Imagine and visualize and see it happening in your life. Get excited about it as though it's already here. Our subconscious doesn't know the difference between what is actually happening or what is being dreamt and born, so if we can feel how it feels to already have achieved it, we are helping to actualize it in our lives.

3. Forgiveness is an important key to transformation

Forgiving oneself, and forgiving others, is paramount in moving forward in our lives. Being unforgiving keeps us stuck in the muck of the past. Remember, that to forgive does not mean condoning bad behavior. It simply means to free yourself from bitterness or harboring resentment. This is easier said than done, but if you want to expand and grow in new ways, don't let the past cast a shadow. If forgiveness seems impossible, you may want to share with wise friends, or seek a counselor.

4. Being grateful helps to transform our lives in positive, beneficial ways

Gratitude is another way to let go of past grievances, and to clear the way for the new. As New Thought musician, Jami Lula, wrote: "I have so much more to be grateful for than to be sorry for." Being thankful raises our vibration of positive change and transformation in our lives. If you haven't felt the power of gratitude for yourself, begin writing five things you are grateful for, for 40 days as the minister suggested to me many years ago. You will be pleased to see and feel a shift from sadness or anger to happiness and more joy. Being joyful will help you on your path of transformation.

5. Allow yourself to step out of your comfort zone

A really essential step in expansion is to try something new, to let yourself experiment with a new way of being. It is so crucial to expansion to be brave and courageous in order to support your new intention. And it is much easier to keep doing the same things; to be content in a comfortable life, to not want to change or disrupt the status quo. But if you are committed to expansion and transformation, this step is usually mandatory. It can be scary, but as I shared, I watched it work beautifully in my own path of expansion.

6. Letting go of fear, anxiety or worry aka TRUSTING

As you become braver and are ready to step out of your comfort zone to try new things, it's really essential to trust that you are being guided. After all, in the first step, you listened to your intuition and Higher Self to find your new mission for expansion. So step out in trust and realize that the Universe has your back! You wouldn't have heard your next step, you wouldn't have been nudged to get out of your comfort zone if you weren't ready to hear it. Go ahead and ride the wave of newness in your life. Like a surfer, you will get better at all of this with practice, practice, practice! Know in your heart of hearts that you are guided and protected, because you always are.

7. The adage "Try, try again" is so true

It is often stated by people who have expanded their lives that failure is a positive thing. If you have been brave, stepped out of your comfort zone in faith, and you try something and it feels like you failed, try again. Like a surfer who falls off the surfboard and is tumbled by the power of the ocean, get up on your expansion surfboard again and ride.

There is almost always beneficial learning when things don't seem to be working out just right. If that happens (and failure doesn't have to happen) then examine the situation, and try, try again. The most amazing inventors, such as Thomas Edison, had countless failures before they discovered something new. Our world would be a lot darker without Edison's light bulb. I am thankful he persevered!

For the greater part of my life, I have practiced all of these steps, not necessarily in this exact order. We each have unlimited potential within us. I believe each of us is a unique and precious part of life. I invite you to discover your growing edge, what you came here to be, and to grow, evolve and transform in magnificent ways!

"The spiral of life is upward. Evolution carries us forward, not backward. Eternal and progressive expansion is its law and there are no breaks in its continuity." ~Ernest Holmes

ABOUT THE AUTHOR: DEBORAH PERDUE

Deborah Perdue, RScP, is the author of *Grace of Gratitude Journal.* She has been a licensed practitioner at the Centers for Spiritual Living since 2007. Her mission statement: *"Knowing the Oneness of God, I broadcast love, beauty, wisdom and joy through my writing, my art, my teaching and counseling as a shining example to all."*

She teaches transformative workshops, classes and facilitates retreats on the topics of gratitude, joy and peace, and how to bring them more fully into our lives. She writes on those same topics online, in her own blog, as well as in local newspaper articles and ezines. She sends out Daily Gratitude Affirmations through the Grace of Gratitude website.

Ms. Perdue is also an accomplished book designer (she designed this book's cover), and is an avid nature photographer. She lives in the country of Southern Oregon with her husband and dogs. Websites are http://www.graceofgratitude.com and http://www.illuminationgraphics.com . She can also be reached at 541-862-7021, and offers spiritual counseling by phone or by Skype.

Chapter 17

Love and Belief: The Roots of all Expansion

By LouAnn Stropoli

There was a time in my life when life was easy. Opportunities for using my gifts came natural. Friendships were plentiful. Life was good. Life was fun.

Life didn't stay that way, however. After many losses and trials I found myself without hope and without love. I fell into isolation. I fell into depression. Not only had my dreams fallen apart but I lost the ability to dream at all.

If life had stayed hopeless, I may not have survived. I knew something had to change and I knew this change was not going to come from the outside. I knew it had to come from deep within. I had to find my will to live again, to dream again, to love again.

It's that part of the story that I want to share with you today. I want you to have access to the pieces that turned my life around. They are the pieces that have allowed me to expand from a grief-stricken hopeless woman to one who has recovered her ability to dream big dreams and live life to its fullest. They are the pieces that took me from victim to business owner, who now delights in helping women reach their highest potential. The two main pieces I used to change my life are these: I learned to fully love myself and then I learned to believe. Below is how I did this. My hope is that these tools will inspire and empower you to rise far above your wildest dreams, take charge of your life, and live every moment to its fullest expression.

I Learned to Fully Love Myself

The most effective change that turned my life around was my awakening towards my own value, purpose, gifts, and uniqueness. I had always been determined to reach my goals. I graduated well, attended good schools, and succeeded at the things that captured my heart. When I went through my darkest days, however, I lost the self-love that I previously had. In fact, I sunk so far down that I wondered if I had ever really fully loved and believed in myself. This was a crucial discovery that changed my life.

There is a fantastic rise of our internal energy and the energy we display for others when we choose to love ourselves fully. When we love ourselves we are less reactionary in life. We're also better able to respond criticism. In fact, we're able to use it to our advantage. When we love ourselves, we are able to love all those other beings around us – foibles and all.

Now I expect that you wouldn't even be reading this book if you didn't love yourself at a significant level. You wouldn't desire to expand your life if you didn't believe in yourself. In fact, I believe you're a big dreamer and you believe you can achieve your goals. If you're human, however, there may still be a small fraction of you that struggles with your self-love or your belief. It's to that small fraction that I'd like to speak today. When we pull out that hidden piece and strengthen it, the influence of our lives is freed to expand beyond anything we could have imagined. The big question before us is this, "How?" How do we learn to love ourselves more fully?

Identify Your True Identity

Who are you? In a culture that honors success, money, fame, and power it's easy to make the mistake of attaching our identity to our jobs or roles in society. When we do this, we suffer from a deep loss of our own ability to enjoy and expand our lives from our deepest values. Sudden shifts in our lives can cause us turmoil. If we're currently working a job that is not our dream or if we lose our employment; if the partner of our dreams gets distracted and ends up in the hands of someone else; if we want children and haven't had the joy of holding our baby – when things like this happen, we can easily fall into a deep valley of the heart. The biggest reason these things throw us off is because we mistakenly wrap our identity around them.

Reorienting ourselves to our true identity is specific to each one of us. My understanding of my truest and deepest identity may not resonate with you or yours with me. That's OK. If we base our identity on the values and beliefs of someone else, then it won't help us to love ourselves more. It would only feel incongruent with our minds and our values. We must love ourselves as we truly see ourselves. For me, my truest identity is this:

I have been created with wonder, love, and beauty and have been gifted in the most perfect ways in order to bring my unique blessings to the world.

When I choose to remember that my identity is rooted in this understanding, then my job or career, the people who choose to love and value me , or not, nor the level of luxury in which I live has any power over my self-love and deep-rooted joy and contentedness. When I find life's challenges trying to uproot me and cause anxiety or fear in my spirit, I deliberately return to the truth of my real identity. Given my unique and magnificent identity, being able to love myself and experience all life has to offer is beyond question. It will be the same for you too.

Reflect: What is the root of your true identity? Can you name it? _____

_____

Forgive Yourself

There are certain experiences in life when we are hit by unexpected curve balls. When these surprises hit us we don't always respond the way we would prefer. Sometimes we make mistakes that hurt others or we let them down. These times can be especially painful when the other person is someone we deeply love. There are also times when we hurt ourselves. We fumble in salary negotiations or we miss the chance to say 'I love you' to a loved one before it's too late. We have all kinds of reasons why we hold unforgiveness towards ourselves. This dip in self-forgiveness carries a heavy burden on our hearts. It blocks our ability to allow ourselves to soar towards the most expanded life possible. Our inner consciousness becomes convinced that we don't deserve the very best in life. We can hold ourselves captive by refusing to allow ourselves grace and forgiveness.

Imagine that it was your best friend who missed the mark in whatever area it is that is holding you back. If your close friend came to you to share this with you, what would you say to her? Would you hold her captive for years or would you comfort her and encourage her to move on? Can you picture yourself right now, talking to your friend? If yes, then mimic that same tone and those same words and speak them to yourself now. Speak them again and again using a loving and caring tone each time. Give yourself the grace you would give any other person. It's only when we can give love and grace to ourselves that we can live our lives to their fullest extent. You may find it helpful to locate a guided for-giveness mediation online. I've found a few that I really like and use often. One note before moving on: If you're like me, then self-forgiveness is something you will want to do on a regular basis. It's like eating. We need regular refreshment to stay on track.

Reflect: For what do you need to forgive yourself? When will you set aside the time to begin?

_____

_____

_____

That's the first part of the equation. Love yourself fully by identifying your true identity and by forgiving yourself. The second major principle that is helping me to expand my life to my largest dreams is belief.

I Learned to Believe

When I was young I was extremely tenacious. Whatever it was that I wanted I went after it. I just naturally focused and achieved my goals. After my dark days, however, I had to learn to believe again. There's really no hope if there's no belief. With no hope or belief, there really is no life. I mean there's existence. Existence, however, is not life. In this next section, I'll share the tips I learned to increase my belief and lead myself to a more expanded and full life.

Influence your Inner Conversation

The most powerful area for developing belief is your inner conversation and your subconscious mind. When we are able to influence ourselves and develop the internal belief that our dreams are possible and inevitable, nothing can hold us back from them. You've heard all the famous quotes like:

"Keep your dreams alive. Understand to achieve anything requires faith and belief in yourself, vision, hard work, determination, and dedication. Remember all things are possible for those who believe." ~ Gail Devers

"It's the repetition of affirmations that leads to belief. And once that belief becomes a deep conviction, things begin to happen." ~ Muhammad Ali

We know and trust the concept of belief. The question is how to develop this aspect of our character even when our lives show no signs of expansion. Increasing your belief, even when life looks dark, isn't an unobtainable miracle. It's simply a matter of doing the right things consistently. Here are a few tools to help you.

Remind Yourself Often

This is probably the most important thing you can do. When I was at my lowest place in life (my only true family members had passed on, my finances were dwindling to zero, and my life looked as bleak as ever), I found every possible method to remind myself that life wasn't over and that I had a future. One of my goals was to move to Sunny SoCal (Southern California) from the Snowy Northeast. In order to achieve this I took time to visualize what life would be like living in the sunshine. I felt the sun on my face and the joy of living a fulfilled life. I let myself feel that free feeling of not having financial concerns. In what was the present I transported myself into the future that I wanted. I know sit here writing this chapter from SoCal!

Now you may know all the neuroscience behind visualization. For a reminder (in a very simplified form) I invite you to think about this: Let's imagine you are heading out to buy a new car. You decide you want a red one. You begin thinking about your new red car, imagining yourself driving your new red car, dreaming about owning your new red car. Finally you buy your new red car. Eventually all you see are red cars all over the place! No blue ones or white ones. You see red ones. Now what's happening here? Well, when you focused on wanting your new red car you told your subconscious mind that it should find more red cars. Your subconscious mind is obedient to what you tell it. It doesn't know the difference between good and bad focus. It simply listens to your focus and finds whatever you are telling it to find. This is important and is exactly why focusing on your fears are anxieties is especially unhelpful. Whatever holds your focus will capture the antenna of your subconscious.

What does that have to do with beliefs? Well, what is it that you want to expand in your life? Do you want to move, change jobs, start a business, meet your spouse, repair your relationships, etc...? Whatever it is, when you take time to focus your thoughts on that goal and imagine all the wonderful aspects of achieving it your subconscious listens and gets to work finding it for you. Let's say you want to change jobs. You start imagining (visualizing) and focusing on the kind of job you want. When you begin your search you might not find any openings. Then, after you train your subconscious for a short while you mysteriously begin to find new options in many locations. You want to remind yourself of your goal as often as possible and in as many ways as possible. I have alarms that go off on my phone throughout the day. Many of those alarms contain reminders to take a few seconds to visualize or focus on my next goal. In order to live an expanded life, we must remind ourselves often of where we want to go.

Reflect: On what goal do you want to focus your imagination? When and how will you do this?

_____

_____

_____

Expand your Courage

I know it's the right thing to do because I feel excited and yet want to throw up.

I must admit I have a natural bent for adventure. Skydiving, rappelling, hanging off cliffs, and public speaking are all great interests of mine. I like adventure in its typical form. There are other areas, however, that excite other people and horrify me. For instance, large group network gatherings and cocktail parties have never been listed as my favorite activities. If I want to grow in my courage, which do you think I need to do more of? Yes, I need to hang out in the bar talking to folks more.

Why does courage help us believe? Think about this: what happens to your overall confidence level when you step out and do something that normally causes you to feel uncomfortable? Each time you do that new thing you get stronger don't you? When your confidence grows and you move past your fears and anxieties you also develop the ability to entertain dreams that are bigger and scarier than ever before. The deepest level of being able to dream is being able to believe the dream is possible.

As our confidence grows so does our ability to believe. This belief-builder technique works even if the uncomfortable things you practice have no direct correlation to your goals. You simply need to reinforce and build your confidence in as many ways as possible.

If you want your life to expand far beyond anything you've ever thought possible, then you want to continue to expand your courage and confidence in new ways. Keep growing and keep building your courage. That is, after all, how our lives expand, one moment at a time.

Reflect: What can you do today or in the next 1-2 weeks to expand your courage?

_____

_____

_____

Reframe Roadblocks as Beautiful Curves in the Journey

Have you ever had life suddenly direct you down an unexpected detour? You're moving along quite nicely minding your own business. Then suddenly you see those flashing yellow lights, barricades, and police cars. Ugh! You didn't leave room in your plan for a detour. Begrudgingly you take the turn simply because you must. What you find on the new road, however, are some of the most interesting views you've ever seen: creatively built homes, kids playing joyfully at the park, and wild flowers displaying their beauty.

Life is like this. Most people won't intentionally take the side roads of life. We like to set our goals and head for them as deliberately as possible. When life throws us unexpended roadblocks it is initially very scary. These roadblocks can be a loss of employment/friend/ business partner or the attraction of our teens towards prescription drugs. Some of life's roadblocks are very scary. They all carry disappointment. When handled with calmness and focus, however, we can use roadblocks for what they really are, beautiful curves in our journey through life. Every portion of our life's journey has something beautiful for each one of us. When we use those curves to the fullest availability, we expand our lives. We can choose to be blocked or we can choose to use our roadblocks as detours meant to lead us to new and magnificent manifestations of beauty. The choice is yours to make

Reflect: What roadblock are you currently turning into beautiful curves in your journey?

_____

_____

_____

Conclusion

Life is a magnificent, beautiful, fascinating, and challenging journey. Each and every one of us desires to live life to its fullest extent. We desire to expand our opportunities, our experiences of love, and ourselves as largely as we possibly can. By learning to love yourself fully and learning to fully believe again you will open doors to a life that is far beyond what you ever thought possible. You will enjoy new opportunities and you will spread your blessing and love to the farthest corners of your existence. Expand your life by loving yourself more and increasing your belief. When you do you will be able to spread your gifts and your blessings to all those within and beyond your reach. The world is waiting for you. The time is now.

ABOUT THE AUTHOR: LOUANN STRIPOLI

LouAnn is a Life and Leadership Coach, Inspirational Speaker, and the Founder of Inspirational Leading Academy. Through Inspirational Leading, LouAnn focuses on helping each and every woman learn to be the best leader she can be in her home, community and workplace. She believes that every woman is a leader as each woman has at least one person looking to her for inspiration.

LouAnn's leadership background includes experience in the musical, spiritual, corporate, and academic realms. She's focused much of her energy over the years learning to lead herself and encourages others to begin at that foundational level.

LouAnn is passionate about helping women create focus, energy, and strength in their lives. She accomplishes this through one-on-one and group coaching, through speaking engagements, and through online programs, which help her reach out to women and aspiring young leaders all around the world. LouAnn would love to connect with you. She can be reached via her website (www.louannstropoli.com) or on any of her social media sites.

Chapter 18

The Secret of the Four Ps and Living Your Dreams

By Shel-lee Davis

The one thing that I found in my life was that no matter how many times I set goals, wrote affirmations, and decided to force myself towards success, I was easily derailed. I could not grow into the person I knew I was supposed to be. It just was not working. Every time I set a goal it seemed to guide my focus to what I did not have. Goals like, I want to lose weight, I want to make more money, I want to be a better person, all focused my attention on I am fat, I don't have the money I need when I need it, somehow I am failing as a person because I am not "good enough". And we all know that what we set attention on we attract into our lives. So I gained weight, struggled with finances, and did not make friends. I was stuck in the cycle of setting goals, failing to reach them and then beating myself up!

The Problem with Goals

Here is my problem with goals. Think about it. When setting goals what am I looking to accomplish? My goals always seemed focused on obtaining or achieving something I didn't have yet. I was always moving away from things I did not want. Even well crafted goals, specific, measurable, attainable, realistic, and time bound. Even goals that were turned into positive affirmations, written out, read every day. Goalsetting for me always seemed to be an affirmation of what I did not have or could not do yet. And rather than advancing forward, they were the glue that held me back.

I knew there had to be a way to live up to my full potential. I knew there had to be a better way to get where I wanted to go. So, I set out to find an alternative to goal setting.

An Alternative to Goal-Setting

So, if setting goals doesn't work, how was I expected to create growth and change? How could I make progress towards my dreams? The answer, I found, lies in discovering what will pull me forward towards the desired outcomes.

A few things it is not.

It is not willpower. Willpower is commonly understood to be the ability to control your thoughts and behaviors in order to achieve something. Willpower requires energy and therefore suffers from depletion and fatigue.

It is not passion. Passion is any powerful or compelling emotion or feeling. Urbandictionary.com defines passion as when you put more energy into something than is required to do it. Passion burns hot and soon burns out.

And it is not planning. Wikipedia defines planning as the process of thinking about and organizing the activities required to achieve a desired goal. Planning often becomes an all consuming end in itself and prevents us from ever moving forward.

The antidote to the failure of goal-setting is purpose. When I finally discovered this and focused on discovering my purpose – which wasn't easy – and wrapped my "goals" in that purpose everything changed. Don't despair, I'm going to share with you steps that you can take, now, today, to uncover the driving purpose that you have within yourself – that will change everything.

Just know, every aspect of my life has changed since I became fully aligned with being on purpose with my choices, my actions, and my direction. My guiding voices come alive.

In the past, I was that person looking for answers using my brain. I attended all of the classes and all of the seminars. I practiced all the strategies. I invested tens of thousands of dollars and thousands of hours, but nothing gave me peace of mind. When I finally looked with my heart, when I listened to my inner wisdom, my still small voice, I found my purpose.

My purpose is to create joy in the lives of everyone I touch, including myself.

When I start here, from joy, to create joy, to generate joy within myself, and within others, everything becomes easy. Then my life flows and a world is created where wonderful things keep showing up.

I look for joy in my personal life, my business life, my physical life, my emotional and intuitional life and my spiritual life. And this guides my actions, my choices, my being and my growth.

The Secret of Purpose

To find my purpose I have to get out of my head. The way to do that is to ask myself a series of questions and as I dig deeper and the answers no longer come quickly and easily from my brain, they start coming from my inner voice which is seated in my heart.

For example, I recently took on the challenge to be in better physical shape. I have been diagnosed with an autoimmune disease. It has caused fused bones and other limitations in my body and I couldn't do things the exact same way that everyone else does or even the same way as I had in the past. I felt compelled to make change.

Next, I chose to see health from the perspective of my life purpose, to live in joy. As I stood in the energy of my purpose,

I was drawn to a three-day SEALFIT Academy. I signed up, and I had not even started working out yet! I began by working out five minutes each day. I grew that to 10 minutes each day. Now, just five months later, I am a successful graduate of the 3-Day SEALFIT Executive Academy, an on-site residential immersion program which focuses on Forging Mental Toughness © through challenging body, mind, emotions, intuition and spirit. I would not have believed this to be possible!

The shift that it took, for me, was to wrap everything into my purpose. And then checking in periodically to make sure that what I was doing was still centered on my purpose. On the first day of the Academy I questioned whether I had taken on too great a task. I got stuck in my head as I saw people who were much more fit showing up. I almost walked away. Instead I checked in with my heart. I had a friend help me through the process of tying my actions to my purpose. Amazingly, as he asked me the questions about what was important to me about completing the Academy, I went from the totally intellectual answer "to prove to myself I can do it" to my heart's answer, "to be present, to do good in the world, to experience wild-eyed childlike joy". And that is what I did at the Academy. The strengths and weaknesses of each member created an unbeatable team. Hooyah!

When my purpose is at the center of each and every action I take, then, my world just opens up to me!

Here is what I do, because the process is really something you can take on too. You can begin to feel more joy and expansion in every area of your life – starting with uncovering and discovering the purpose within you.

This is so different from the plain setting of external goals. It never worked for me to try and bootstrap my way into staying on track. Now my purpose draws me forward effortlessly.

How to Go About Finding Your Purpose

Finding your purpose is so simple that it can be difficult. For me, the process started with looking at the things that were working in my life. I made a list of three to five things that I felt good about doing. Eating well – no sugar, helping people find the home of their dreams, spending time with my nieces, breakfast with my husband each day. Then one, by one, I asked myself the questions, questions I had learned from my mentor, Joe Stumpf.

What is important about not eating sugar? I avoid empty calories. And what is important about not eating empty calories? Empty calories don't fuel my body. What's important about fueling my body? It gives me energy. And what is important about having energy? I can help more people. Question and answer, seven to nine levels deep. I get to touch more lives. I get to help people live into their dreams. It makes them happy. I create a space for joy in their lives. It gives me joy. There it is, my purpose, **to create joy in the lives of everyone I touch, including myself.**

As we like to say in my family when we do things over and over again: Then just "rinse and repeat" with every item on your list. I am always amazed that, when I dig deep, things as different as the work I love and having breakfast with my husband get me into the same space, my purpose, Joy!

Ask yourself the question seven to nine times. It takes four or five levels for most people, including me, to get out of the head and into the heart. Then it takes more probing, to the point where the answers don't come easy, to get to your purpose.

When I get stuck, I will say, "Well if you did know, what would it be?" Or, I will think of what would happen if I did not do that important thing, like if I did not help more people, what would happen to them, and then I ask myself again, "What is important about helping more people to you?" Both of these methods work well to get me unstuck and move the process forward. Sometimes it helps to have someone else ask the questions. But they must only ask the questions and be silent, while your heart searches for the answer.

CAUTION! If you are not finding this convergence as you go through your list, then dig deeper. Don't let yourself off the hook. Get to the big emotion, the big why, that is the focus of the things that are working in your life. THIS IS YOUR PURPOSE. Take the time to find it.

Here are some examples of purpose that have been shared with me by clients and friends. – To insure my family's safety

– To always be my best me – To walk with God – To have financial freedom. Your purpose will be as individual as you. Embrace it and use it to fuel your dreams.

Keep in mind that Purpose remains consistent over time, changing slowly or not at all. My purpose when I was in financial and personal strife was to "create peace of mind". This purpose remained with me for many years. It changed when I substantially created peace of mind in my life. It opened the door to my current purpose of "joy".

Small Steps Lead to Big Things

I look at my life each quarter and figure out where I would like to see change and growth. When I take on the rest of my life a slice at a time, absolute change is possible and it starts so easily. Each quarter, I choose three areas of my life to concentrate on for that quarter. This last quarter, I chose my business, my physical health, and my nutrition.

In my business, I had chosen to double the number of people that I help each year. I've been serving about 20 people each year, and I set out to help 40 people this year. Change was going to be required to happen for this to occur, and I was open to that change.

In my physical health, I chose to increase my fitness. I had turned into a couch potato. I saw this in a measurable outcome, like getting my body fat under 30 percent.

In my nutrition, I chose to keep information about foods that were creating a negative response in my body. My body has sensitivities, and by becoming more aware of what foods fuel my body and what foods create problems, I can proactively use food to increase my health.

Expansion in My Business

The first question I asked myself about serving 40 people this year was "what is important about that to me?" The intellect answered immediately, I would make more money. What's important about that? I could help more people. So if I make more money and help more people what does that do for me? It would give me a sense of financial freedom. Question again, I would have no worries.

Then I began to arrive in a place that is difficult, beyond money, beyond helping people, beyond freedom, beyond no worries. What is important about this to me? At the fifth level of this question, I realized that I desire to be very present with the people I am serving with my business skills. I desire to be wholly present and available with all of me in all my life's interactions.

Now, what is important about this?

And as I am getting deeper and deeper, I am getting very, very quiet. And then, like a clash of thunder it hits me. Because I want to hear them from the heart, not just the words they are saying, but truly communicate heart to heart.

Now, as I go deeper, even below this, and behind this, and underneath this desire, I realize I would like to instigate and create and generate joy not only in my life, but in the lives of those people I am serving with my skills. Back to my purpose.

Expansion in My Health and My Nutrition

I begin the process fresh with my health. I begin to ask myself the questions, and then I ask more questions to dig deeper! What is important about being stronger and more fit? Because when I'm fit I am happy and I am joyful. If I take it seven to nine levels, I end up with happy, comfortable and joyful. What is important about tracking my food sensitivities? It becomes all about the comfort of knowing what I can eat and not have a reaction so I can let go of this limiting factor, and become happy and joyful. Back to my purpose.

Purpose is Different for Everyone

At one point I doubted myself. How could something as simple as joy be my life's purpose.

Like magic I was introduced to the character Joy in the book The Energy Bus! She introduced the thought that the creation of a better world results from the impact of each person's presence, joy and positive actions. That really says it for me. If I can share my joy with others, this gives me even a greater sense of joy, and the world gets better one touch at a time.

Whatever your purpose, share it with the world.

The Science of Being

In the past, I felt compelled to take on 10, even 20 "goals" at a time. That just led to overwhelm and stagnation. The wonderful thing is purpose creates focus.

Real change began to happen when I took on my life in slices that were completely possible to manage. I found that I attract different people. I find people that are happy, that would like to be happier. I have learned that when you know your purpose, this sends that message to the universe, and then more wonderful people show up to fulfill your purpose.

I observe that when I am joy, on purpose, living a joy-filled life, I am able to relax and trust my knowing. I am pulled into abundance. My world expands to make room for more changes that I am fully conscious are on track and in alignment with my higher self.

Using Purpose to Pull You Forward

Let's use my business expansion as an example.

I choose one thing that will move me closer to the joy. The thing I chose recently in my business was to double the number of people I help each year. I am clear that if I connect directly and speak with about three people, two will choose to work with me. So, I created a performance measure of face-to-face appointments. I became clear that should I have face-to-face appointments with about 60 people in a given year, 40 people will choose to work with me.

Then I look for a system, a Process, that will create this for me. I chose two processes – the first is an automated system to reach out to my past clients on a regular basis. Because it is automated someone else can run that for me. The second is an automated system to reach out to people who don't know me yet and offer them valuable information about our area and home values. Again, once fully operational, someone else can run this for me.

Now I am free to create face-to-face meetings with people and create joy in the lives of my past and new clients. I'm not in a struggle to continuously find new clients. I simply have things all in alignment so I can meet with my clients. And that is the change I want to see in my business or what I call "the Profit" or product.

This is how it happens:

- Know your Purpose

- Identify the change you want to see – the Profit

- Define the Performance Measure

- Put a Process into Place

- Enjoy the Profit

• Live in your Purpose

I call this my "4 Ps" and it's really a lot of fun for me.

• Purpose

• Performance Measure

• Process

• Profits

Ease!

These are my 4 Ps for living big. I use my 4 Ps every day. I evaluate all my opportunities around my purpose and apply my 4 Ps. I ask questions about the Profit I would like to see this quarter. Profit does not always mean money. It is the change we want to see. For me it is helping people, choosing nutrition, being fit.

Then I create different Performance Measures for different slices of my life where I am asking for change. What one or two simple things will have a direct impact on the Profit.

Lastly, I identify at least one Process get me there. I look for one simple system that I can establish and often delegate to someone else to maintain.

I often do this on a day-to-day basis when faced with a project that is difficult ... what is important about this? I wrap everything in my purpose. Helping people give and receive joy, my purpose, enriches what I originally started out to accomplish, my profit. And between the purpose and the profit I build the ladder of performance measures and process, things I can actually see, accomplishments I can measure. And I focus on one or two things in just three areas of my life each quarter. Purpose creates focus. Believe it or not, I once chose a performance measure to only check my emails 3 X per day. That was the first year I helped 20 people. I wasn't getting to the 20, something was distracting me, preventing me from getting there? You think emails, really, but it worked. My process was to inform my clients and associates that I respond to emails within six hours. That allowed me to check only three times per day.

The Magic

Well it really isn't magic, but it sure feels that way. I keep things simple. I wrap my profits, my choices, my decisions in my purpose. I check in regularly to make sure what I am doing still resonates with my purpose. And I grow exponentially as a result.

Let the magic of the 4 Ps work for you.

ABOUT THE AUTHOR: SHEL-LEE DAVIS

Shel-lee Davis jokes that she was born into a family of gypsies. She moved so often that the only constant in her life was change. And she seemed to thrive on it.

As a child, Shel-lee developed a knack for self-counsel, looking inside for answers and guidance. Paying attention to the still small voice that was always there when needed. This was a benefit since in the whirlwind of her childhood, a childhood of seemingly perpetual motion that took her halfway around the world and back, twice by the age of 10, friendships were hard to form. By the time she entered the 9th grade, at the ripe old age of 14, her family had lived in 12 different places. Shel-lee is quick to point out they she did not move so often because her parents were in the military. The family moved because her dad was always looking for a better life for his family, chasing his elusive dreams.

As an adult, Shel-lee created her own state of perpetual motion to emulate her childhood. Over the years she has embraced several careers, mostly focused on finance. Bookkeeper for a property management company. Scheduler for a grading and paving contractor. Several financial positions in the construction industry. Project Manager for several small construction jobs. Controller and Budget Director for a land development company.

Then moving into the accounting world, holding positions as a manager and partner of the Litigation and Insolvency department at Newport Beach accounting firm and a director in the same area at a Los Angeles based accounting firm. During this period she found herself very outward-focused and the guiding voices that had steered her growth and brought her so much joy as a child were silent.

Shel-lee Davis is the author of an article on insolvency *"When It All Comes Tumbling Down"* published in the Recovery Advisor. She is also the author of *The End of the American Nightmare: Unveiling the simple secrets to solving your home and mortgage dilemma* published in 2012. She is a Certified Practitioner of Neuro Linguistic Programming.

Today, Shel-lee has reconnected with her still small voice and happily helps people find the joy of home ownership as a real estate consultant in Palos Verdes, California and surrounding beach cities.

Chapter 19

Are You Ready?
By Stina Devi Eriksson

I live in a small town in the middle of Sweden called Hudiksvall. Not much happens. We have winter with snow and we have summer and go to the beach and have ice cream. I like it most of the time.

Most of my life has been a search. When I was a child, I talked to all entities, all animals and bodies. I was a healer from the start. Then, oh then, the mind became my quest. My open heart was met with fear and I was shunned. I could not understand. How could I conceive of such acts? I moved into my mind and hid there. I put the Knowing of my soul on pause. Actually I shunned the part of me that was not received with love. Not until about 30 years later did I realize that it is not the Mind OR the Soul - they are entwined and I am all. Everything.

The journey back to my true self began after a traumatic event. I had fallen deeply in love with a young man that I was certain would be my love forever. I had in my mind set up well most of my life and made plans. The kids, the dog and the house and you know... everything that was supposed to happen so that I would be just the same as everyone else, and ok. I´d be home free and then I would finally get back to heaven and be at peace. If I could only make a life with as little effort and suffering as possible. However, it didn´t turn out that way. He was killed in a car crash and I was left on Earth with no clue whatsoever.

After some time I came into contact with Reiki, which led me to become a Reiki Master Teacher. I began to know and see how energy shifted in people. I began to receive again. Messages. I received this wonderful message from my deceased boyfriend:

"I am the wind that whispers in your ear.

That tickles you on the neck. That cools you in the summer heat.

I am the sun's rays that wink at you, that shine on you.

That warm up the cold darkness inside you.

I am always close to you. I hold you in the night my love.

I am always here for you, never doubt that and never question that. I love you.

Just because you cannot see me or touch me does not mean you cannot feel my presence.

When you feel joy I am there smiling with you. When you cry I feel your sadness

and I hold you in my loving arms. I know you miss me, but I have never left you.

We will meet again and time is not as long as you believe it to be, it´s merely a moment.

Live your life and love, that is all that matters. Take this opportunity!

Love yourself as well my dear because you are amazing. Don´t fear. There is no one here judging you. You cannot fail. God loves YOU too.

All the forces of the Universe are here for you. Ask and you shall receive.

Live your dream and we will assist you. Always. Never doubt that.

Imagine a bubble around your body with light energy.

Don't let anything or anybody break down your faith in us, the other side.

As long as you believe and have faith there is no miracle too great.

Everything is possible, my little butterfly.

Surround yourself with friends, become your own friend.

I will never abandon you, and neither will God

AMEN"

Receiving this channeled message was really weird to me because I knew it was just something else. I had never just written something down like that. And I had chills all over my body. I knew it was real. But it wasn't until very much later that I could really feel that it was true for me.

The Marriage

I knew something else was possible. I had felt the energy. I knew there was love so much greater than the hurt of the loss. Yet I continued to stay trapped in my mind. I felt like I could not trust this new awareness and I went back into my mind that had become my ally. It was supposed to get the message and tell me so I could hide my bleeding heart away, so that I could stay safe and just make it: the one answer that was going to keep me from being hurt again. I set it up so that if I could figure out how the heck he could be so unkind to leave me in this awful place and just go die like that, then so I could know what to avoid and how to go about everyday without ever meeting such sorrow again. What did I do wrong? Did I do something to create this? Was I so wrong? Questions like that kept me wandering in the deep sea of sorrow.

I began diving into self-help books, I became a vampire for New Age material. I read everything, took classes, bought into this and that. I ended up, well frankly, insane. My mind had no answer and my heart was still bleeding. I still tried to cover up and hold back all the sorrow.

Then one day I laid down my weapons and The Mind and The Soul agreed to spend their life together for good times and for bad. I realized that the mind could only do so much for me and that I could actually choose to acknowledge the Me I knew I was. All of it. In the space of love, compassion and allowance. So here I am. And now I want to share with you a little bit about the Energy of Expansion, of getting out of your own constructs and limitations and how wonderfully at ease you can feel in the midst of all that Life offers. Welcome!

Stress, distress and contraction...

...is the opposite of expansion. If you are stressed you are basically in your mind. Your mind is a collector of all the thoughts and conclusions you at one point or another believed was a great idea to keep as it would lead you to, if not more happiness, then at least less suffering. We all do that. Unless you are already enlightened, but then you wouldn't be reading this in the first place. Distress is when the stressors become unhealthy keeping you from exploring and living life. It can be thoughts like "I am not good enough", "My mom said I am too lazy so I could never make this work" or "I am to fat/thin/broke/alone" or whatever comes to mind for you.

All of these thoughts come up because you had consciously or unconsciously kept them or created them. **Thoughts like these create contraction and limitations and you become just like those who told you the lies in the first place.** Because they are lies. Not in your Mind, but in your Being. If you are aware of what you believe about yourself and others you have come a long way. Being aware is the first step to changing and moving into greater greatness. And now comes the yummy part.

You are Divine Pure Light

Yup. You are. You are a soul infused body walking the Earth for a bit of timespace in order to explore and encounter all that can possibly be beneficial to your Soul's Expansion and Knowing. And yeah, that also includes all that you may perceive as crap along the way. This includes a loss of a loved one, a difficult birth, losing your job, divorce, becoming overweight, fighting with your kids over dinner. Well that list can go on and on – and it is a part of everything that is right now. When I talk to the Angels, or as I would say, to parts of me that are not in this realm, parts that I have access to, they show me how the Light of the Universe pours into my head like a thick honey-like glowing glittering energy. At Birth it filled my entire body and it is still there. The connection, the bond was created.

As we move along, we, by believing and acting in unskillful ways (I will come back to this later), this light seems jaded when looking at it. But that is an illusion because we are still that Light in our being. All the points of views are like band aids we put on our body when we hurt and our path no longer seems so bright and lit up. Pulling those band aids off can at first feel awfully uncomfortable. You may scream, shout, say you´d never do it again, cry or have feelings of aggression or fear. You are becoming aware. This is where some of us go into depression or lose our faith, we create havoc in a way or another, we turn to addiction of sorts or we do whatever we can to not feel anything. We feel disconnected. Lonely. But the Divine never quits. It never stops pouring Divine Light. It never stops the flow from its part no matter what we may believe is true. "I am bad" – and the Divine answers: I love you! "I am wrong I will never succeed" and the Divine answers: I love you!

The Divine/God/The Field

For me, God or the Divine Source is that space that all of us hold within us that knows that there is no goal, there is no right or wrong, I am always Loved, I cannot fail, we are all a part of Oneness, I am never ever alone on any level of my Being. This space is a space of Loving Kindness, of Allowance, of Peace and of Knowing. It is a space where the Present Moment is all there is and by really, really knowing that you relax. You relax fully and you receive. It is a place of Joy that has nothing to do with circumstances.

How do I get there?

The true self is never lost. But sometimes we need to take actions to again reveal to ourselves how awesome we truly are. These are some suggestions you can use:

1. Find out what makes you YOU - what is your uniqueness?

What makes your body go WOW! and your mind go: Really?!? Is this even possible?? What makes the energy shift for you so that you find YOU again? Is it singing? Writing? I would say it is most often engaging in a creative "modality" or at least it is something where you do not use your mind. It is called BEing. Just for the fun of it. So make a list of five things, and whenever you think you are losing it, just pick one of them and do it. Be the truck that runs over that hill and do it no matter what your mind blabs on about. Use your free will.

2. Choose your actions and thoughts consciously

This one can feel a bit tricky and it is. Thus meditating is highly recommended. When you meditate in the most basic way I know, using the Mindfulness of Breathing meditation, then you have nothing else to accomplish. You just breathe. Then the Mind will show up for sure. At first you may think you have gone completely mad, I did. Or perhaps you are already aware and your mind will go blank and put into rest mode and your body will relax. If you spend time meditating you will find that there is no hurry. You become more present. You catch yourself before saying that thing to your spouse/child/co-worker/parent/friend that would hurt them because you feel unseen or unheard. You will stop and you will know that the outcome will not benefit either of you.

All actions and all thoughts are choices. We find that when the intention is skillful, that of Loving kindness and Knowing, there will be no separation born out of it. When we are coming from unskillful intention of hate and ignorance or that which causes harm, you perceive duality. These concepts are taken from Buddha Dharma, or Buddhism, and I use them because the illusion of right and wrong is what keeps the Mind going and is not of much use. As we use the terms skillful and unskillful we are able to be in the Moment choosing as we go along. The Buddhist Meditation master Chögyam Trungpa defines "Ignorance" as being ignorant of the present moment. We keep looking for knowledge outside of ourselves, which leaves us completely lost to the Present Moment that has Everything in it if you are only fully present. When we have come to realize the Truths of the soul and no longer strive we can choose consciously and thus in every moment expand as our band aids are gently released by the energy of Loving Kindness. Being present with what is in the moment is being alive, aware, it is being You.

3. Engage in something

We are never separate, yet human beings are quick to shun themselves. We conclude that we are all alone because we think, do or react in a way we judge as bad or wrong. Or we go into superiority mode because we have made it, we have money, we have the bigger car or whichever status measurement we have decided is the top notch. These ways are both the highway into depression, sadness, fear and anger. We are part of Creation and when we decided we are separate, our selves crash. It does not compute and the body goes into protest. It may become ill. The body will tell you, believe me. When this occurs, it is of great importance to hang out with others.

Many of us have bought into the notion that "I" alone create everything in my life... That is walking a thin line my friend. The truth is we are co-creators. You would wish to do some co-creating if you find yourself in this loophole. For me, climbing out of this hole happened when I found a group of people that did not in any way want to change me. I was totally free to feel crappy, they knew that there was something else possible but they used no force to move me into it. No one said to me to not think as I did, do what I did. They just didn´t judge. There are such people in the world. Go find some!

The Energy of Expansion

The energy of expansion? Yes. Did you ever have a problem and the solution came to you just like that and you had that huge sigh of relief? That ease. And the feeling of being supported. The more you move into the energy of expansion, i.e. letting go and being the invitation, the more that feeling will appear in your life. Your life will become a full color experience. It is as if the light has been turned on, your sense of color, smell, touch becomes so sensitive and everything becomes a miracle. You are more present in every movement. You are gracious. You resist nothing. Your doubts will be dropped like taking off an old piece of clothing. You will know that even in the midst of what may seem like a bad thing there is something behind the scenes. Something so loving that would never ever truly hurt you. No longer will you stress about finding the right solution, no, you will be the invitation for the gifts to come to you at the precise moment. You wish. And let go. You ask for. And you let go. And with open arms you are fully and completely alive.

Is it possible? Is it really possible? Yes! Yes!!!!

When you come to the place where you resist nothing, you know – yes you fully truly know that you are always supported. You are never alone. And you are always loved. Resting in this awareness is the key to the energy of expansion. The Light. The Love. The source for Loving kindness. Your energy is a gentle breeze, like sunshine, like a mother's love to a child. It is pure. You are now resting within. You no longer walk your life path trying to avoid anything in your experience. There is no struggle, no judgment, no past to keep, no future to catch. You are now as wide as the Universe and beyond. You are now open to receive all energies. You are One with the Universe. Your expansion is unlimited.

When you are there.... Holy Moly! Pooooof! The Universe comes to you with the most awesome gifts and the level to which you live in Loving Kindness is like floating on a wave. In the sunshine. In the summer. With an ice cream. Best of Luck my friend, and remember, YOU are Awesome!

With Love,

Stina Devi Eriksson, explorer

ABOUT THE AUTHOR: STINA DEVI ERIKSSON

Stina Devi Eriksson is an Energy transformation healer using her own mix of methods uniquely tailored for each client. She says everything is energy and everything can be shifted through the presence of Loving Kindness and allowance. She says it is a matter of feeling connected and perceiving the bigger picture of the True Self that includes so many more levels of us that we are not always aware of.

Writing has always been one of her favourite things to engage in as well as singing. Growing up she always wrote short stories and engaged in music. She continued studying music at University as well as taking classes in creative writing. She later became a sound technichian and played in several bands.

After her boyfriend was badly injured in a motorcycle accident she had an extraordinary experience. As his life support was to be turned off she felt a sudden connection to the Divine and a rush of Love and Light. She found herself sending healing to the soul of the young man in the hospital bed. This awakened her in a new and profound way. During the time of grieving she came into contact with Reiki, an ancient Japanese healing method, in which she later become a Reiki Master Teacher. Teaching Reiki led her to the knowing that we all are connection to Source energy if only we open up to it. The joy of the attendees was immense and the ease and grace created opened Stina's heart to looking for more.

In the fall of 2006 she started studying Bioenergetic therapy healing at Axelsons Gymnastiska Insititute in Stockholm taught by the internationally well-known researcher, teacher, author and previous head master at the University for alternative medicine in St. Petersburg Boris Aranovich. She learned ancient Tao healing techniques, Tibetan healing and ancient Russian healing methods to shift energy in all fields creating dis-ease. She later attended an internship at his company in Stockholm which included learning more about Russian techniques,the use of scanning systems and treatment devices as well as translating manuals for medical devices, systems and information material.

In May 2007 she attended the International Quantum Energy Medicine seminar in Stockholm. Listening to speakers like Dr James Oschman, Mark Abadi, Dr rer.nat. Hartmut Müller and international bestselling authour Lynne McTaggart her interest for energy medicine grew and she decided to study it more extensively.

After practicing for years, studying western medicine and also raising children she started looking for more information about Energy Medicine and in 2010 she graduated top student at The Institute of Bioenergetic and Informational Healthcare (IBIH) in Germany. Classes included teachings of anatomy, physiology, nutrition and laser therapy. Also new methods as biofeedback systems, NLP, EFT and informational medicine as the NES system. Studied also included teachings from the Heart Math Insititute and the research from Dr Bruce Lipton on epigenetics and META-medicine by Dr Hamer.

Before the birth of her third child he had her own business where she offered sessions, meditation groups and classes in healing. Alongside with taking care of the children and working for her husband in his IT-business she enjoys studying anything from neurobiology to consciousness and Buddha Dharma.

Her longing to write lead her to start blogging where she is offering the teachings of the Knowing she receives. She also offers remote healing sessions which have been a huge success with testimonials of her warm heart, gentleness, knowledge and compassion.

Stina says: If a person finds within themselves the Knowing that there is no separation - their connection with Source/God life becomes a flourishing adventure where the heart blooms and thrives. Separation, she continues, is the greatest problem there is in mankind. Love, compassion and kindness is the key to regaining this connection that has never really left us. We have just come to believe it has and that she says is the core of any problem. It is her mission in life to reconnect people with source so that they can live life to the fullest with ease and joy. It is our birthright to receive she says, and when we put up stop signs we shut receiving off. The good news is of course that the signs can be taken down. For more information please visit stinawhitelight.com.

Chapter 20

Expanding You
By Tracey Samlow

*en-er-gy - noun \en-er-jee\ - the strength and vitality
required to sustain physical and mental activity
: the flow of power*

*ex·pan·sion - noun \ik-'span(t)-sh?n\ -
: the act or process of expanding
: the quality or state of being expanded*

As a young a child I saw spirits, heard voices and experienced déjà vu. Of course, no one believed me and, like so many others, I learned to doubt my own experience, dismiss it and relegate it to the basement of disowned energy.

For the next 20 plus years I turned off my natural ability of connecting with a world that exists beyond what we are taught not to even to believe in, let alone see. I stopped seeing spirits and experiencing the world outside of this one. The one we insist is the only one.

I stopped talking about it. I stopped sharing my beliefs and experiences. As a result, I lived a very contracted life and let others lead me, dictate what I should think and feel. I was supposed to live a "good" life (according to others), instead of accepting who I really was (and am).

Then it happened, like the Big Bang. I woke up.

In a moment, this false idea of who I was just collapsed. I had experienced suffering and trauma in my life, and it all started flooding back into my conscious mind. I wept... and wept... and wept. It felt like I had lost everything, including myself.

I didn't know who I was anymore and at that moment I simply gave up and surrendered. I surrendered control and this dysfunctional notion of who I thought I was. The bubble burst and I suddenly awoke to my true nature. Who I really was.

Who am I?

I am a seer. I again can see spirits and have visions that give me strength. I am a gifted connector of hearts and an inspirational teacher. I am here to help others wake up to their true nature. I am the "I AM" that has always been and will always be. I am the silence that I hear and the peace that there is when I close my eyes. And I am here to help you remember that. It is my dharma to be the conduit for anyone else that I may touch to realize that... *We are ONE... always and forever.*

We have the power to experience life as the greatest gift that can be bestowed. We need for nothing. We are already everything we need because we are ONE with the energy that created us. We are not separate from that energy, we **are** that energy.

Everything is energy. That means YOU are energy. Now let's consider what that really means.

Energy grows where energy goes. YOU have the power to expand your energy. Energy is a substance which can be transformed into different forms, but always remains, exactly the same. Pretty cool, huh?

It cannot be created or destroyed. But it can be expanded or contracted.

YOU are energy in the form of a conscious being, a human being. Because you are energy (and you are conscious of it), you have the power (gift really) of being able to convert your energy into different forms.

The process of transforming energy can be perceived consciously, even though it occurs unconsciously. You do not think to think your thoughts. The thoughts just arise. You do not need to make yourself feel emotions. You just do.

Just like you do not think to breathe each breath, or grow hair or digest that yummy pasta you had last night. It all happens all by itself. Of course, without all that happening, your body would convert into a different form of energy. It will break down and become a part of the Earth's energy system.

This simply means that your energy will still exist, but the form will have changed. But **the energy of who you truly are is constant and will never change**. Your form will convert into a new existence and then another and then another. But you... YOU remain.

Think about yourself, your life, and energy in this way...

YOU are pure consciousness connected to all consciousness. You are pure energy connected to all energy. Innumerable forms and one energy. Your physical body is energy. Your thoughts and emotions are energy. Your environment is energy. Same energy, different forms.

You can cooperate with that energy to take action based upon the thoughts and emotions you choose and/or agree with.

Often (actually most of the time) you go about living your life without thinking about the energy that you are and the power that that gives you. You do often stop and consider how your emotional state effects, not only your perceptions of your life, but also all those other beings around you and, indeed, the whole world.

Your entire life is simply a reflection of the energy that you choose to focus on. You do not always recognize that you have the power to expand or contract your life. Recognized or not, that is what you are doing every moment.

Here's a fun way to expand your notions about who YOU are and the energy that YOU are...

Think about your life and everything in it as a movie. You are the writer, producer and director of this movie. It is an epic movie and it's playing on a big, 3D screen. You create the story that you wish to tell, the role all the actors play, the plot, the setting, the locations, the costumes. As the director, your job is to cast and direct the actor that will bring the story of your life... uh... well, to life. Every bit of lighting, every camera angel, all the special effects, all of it. You direct the energy of the story and how the movie goer will perceive that story.

But you are not just the director. You are also an actor in the movie and, most of the time, the main character. You play whatever part that the director wishes you to. And you are in every scene.

The character, of course, changes as the story unfolds. If s/he didn't it would be a really boring movie. As the actor, your job is to pretend to be someone that you are not. You act out the thoughts that the character (if s/he were real) would think, feel all the emotions, all moving the story along, plot, subplot and subtext.

You are a really good actor so you really become the part. You get lost in it. You totally identify yourself with the character. But, despite all the thoughts, feelings, situations and experiences, you are not ever that character. You are an actor, playing out the actions of the character. And you are doing a damn good job of it.

And now it gets even more interesting. You are the audience too. You are the viewer, the movie goer (complete with popcorn and candy). As the viewer, you are an outsider, but, at the same time, totally immersed in the experience. You too are thinking the thoughts and feeling the emotions that the director intended you to feel as you watch the show.

Through effect, illusion and emotional payoffs, you are led to perceive the story in the way that the director wishes. But there is one big difference here. Something within you knows that there is more to the story than what is being played out on the screen. You sense that there is more. You know that there is more.

And, what might that something more be?

Since you are watching the movie, no matter how engrossed you get, you know that you are not in the movie. As you watch, you are able to fully experience the story, the action, the twists and turns. Yet you know that everything happening is an illusion.

The whole movie is an illusion being projected onto a screen that is being perceived by you. That hardball that gets thrown at you in the movie is not going to come through the screen and hit you in the head, while you are sitting in the theatre, chomping on some popcorn. A house burns down, but the screen has not even the smell of fire. The great flood comes and the screen and you remain dry as a bone. The movie is not "real". Fun, interesting, engaging? Yes. But "real", no.

Your life is your movie. All the events that happen within it may feel "real". But it truly is only an illusion.

Take a moment right now and become the audience. Can you observe yourself outside of yourself? Can you see your body in form? Can you feel the emotions and hear the thoughts that you are experiencing while you are observing? Of course. As the audience you are watching the whole thing. I mean, thoughts don't just wander around on their own. You are always the witness to them.

Now ask... who is observing all this? Who is seeing? Who is feeling? Who is hearing? Is it YOU? Are YOU the you that you are viewing, or are YOU the one watching?

How can YOU be the viewer of you? How is it that you able to view your life as an outsider looking in? Who is looking in? If our life is like a movie and you are the director, the actor and the viewer, than who is this viewer of the movie of your life? Who is the director? Who is the actor? How is this possible? What is "real"? Are you "real"?

Or, to put it the way sages and wise ones have put for thousands of years "Who are YOU??"

The truth is that YOU are the viewer. How is it that I can say that? Well, simply this. While the director changes, the part played changes, the story changes, the plot, the setting the characters, the costumes, the viewer doesn't.

The viewer is pure consciousness, pure awareness or as Eckhart Tolle likes to call it, pure presence. This is the energy that is constant and eternal. You are always the viewer. But you can expand into being the director or the actor. But without the viewer, the director and the actor do not exist. They depend on you, the viewer. You do not depend on them.

You, the viewer, watch your life as you create it, just as if it was a movie. But there is no point to creating a movie if there is no one to watch it. Your life simply cannot exist if YOU are not there to view it. The director has no story to tell, and the actor has no part to play. The screen is blank. No popcorn. No candy.

As the viewer, you watch your story unfold and your life *feels* "real". But it isn't. Your life is as dear and engaging and meaningful as it is just a movie. It is not who YOU are. You are way more than the story being told. You are far greater than the character you happen to be playing. YOU are energy that makes it all possible, pure and simple.

Who YOU really, really are is who you has always been and

always will be. Pure consciousness. Pure presence. This is the YOU that just is, the enlightened witness of your body, your thoughts, your emotions and all the experiences that make up your life.

This is the YOU that is present when you close your eyes and sit in silence, when the movie is turned off and the screen is blank. This is the YOU that can be the director and create the story, or be the actor and portray a role.

And this is the YOU that can **choose to identify with the story**, or choose to expand beyond the story. This is the YOU that has the power to turn off the movie.

The energy that YOU are is the only thing that is "real". This is your true being. The reality that you think you are living, whether you think it is wonderful or awful, is an illusion. It's merely how you appear.

When you fall asleep at night and dream, your mind thinks that the dream is real. That is, while you are in it. When you open your eyes you recognize that the dream experience was totally subjective, a play in the mind. Your thoughts and emotions are products of your mind and they are not who YOU are. This is all part of the illusion that YOU experience as the viewer. Just like the movie is a brilliant and entertaining illusion. Thoughts, sensations, emotions, experiences are energy, and because they can be viewed they cannot be YOU.

Who YOU are cannot be viewed. How could you? The eye

cannot see itself. The sharpest knife cannot cut itself. The most sensitive scale cannot weigh itself. The viewer (that's you) cannot see itself.

Being the viewer means that you have the power to expand or contract all states of your being, simply by viewing the possibility of its existence. YOU choose to be the director and create any story that you wish, and it will be. YOU choose to be the actor and expand your reality in every moment by acting out the story line (the vision of possibility) envisioned by the director.

YOU can view your experiences and perceive your life in an infinite variety of ways, but remember that those experiences however grand, are not YOU. The YOU that you are has the power to expand your consciousness beyond the story and experiences that you are currently viewing.

Everything in your life as you experience it is but a projection on the 3D screen of your mind. To know this liberates you from being stuck in any story and empowers you to shift the view at will. The viewer is never forced to sit in the theater.

Remember... YOU are energy. YOU are the power that can expand YOU. Even so, who YOU really really are is constant. It never changes. And, because the same energy takes all forms, YOU are ONE with all.

YOU are not separate from pure consciousness, you *are* pure consciousness. YOU can choose to expand or contract your movie in every moment. So let's start choosing a movie with a happy beginning, middle and... well, there is no end.

NOW go... **e x p a n d** YOU!

ABOUT THE AUTHOR: TRACEY SAMLOW

Tracey Samlow is an inspirational speaker and author, promoter of conscious messengers, Mind, Body and Spirit counselor, and spiritual connector of hearts. She gives guidance on how to simply be in harmony with oneself and the Universe, and her passion is assisting others in waking up to their true nature.

Her life experiences include theatre, art, food, nutrition, hospitality, health, fitness, healing, business, marketing and creating opportunities for others. She is also an entrepreneur and philanthropist who seeks spiritual partnerships where giving back is part of the mission. Tracey devotes her life to increasing consciousness and spreading love around the planet, alongside her two incredible children. Together they live an expansive life filled with grace and miracles. Tracey enjoys sharing knowledge, inspiring others, and reminding us all that we are ONE...always and forever. Connect with Tracey at www.traceysamlow.com.

Chapter 21

The Sticky Road to Glory
By Erica Glessing

It's funny how much I asked for expansion before it came. I look at the road that I took to be in a place where my reality is flowing in generous waves of synchronicity – almost like a dream, life unfolds with grace for me and it certainly did not always feel like that.

The sticky was so much a part of my life, I forgot that the magic of me could be in an expansive state. I look at early 2012, when I first recognized that I was ADD (attention deficit disorder). This was a brilliant moment that changed my life and my capacities, forever. I was coaching a client and bought a book to help me. It was all about distraction, and I took the self-test. Of 124 test questions, I got 87 "right" and knew that my entire life, I had been ADD.

One of the things that is generally re-gurgitated about ADD

is this "if you didn't have it as a child, you don't have it now." The only piece left out is that children who over-achieved and got good grades and were not behavior problems would generally never be identified as a problem. So if your brain operates a certain way, it might be a certain way even if you never knew it as a child.

So fast forward say 50 years and I am recognizing my own brain. This was a beautiful moment, because given my brain, and how it works, I was able to find some wonderful supplements and vitamins and food that work with my brain. I was able to build a business that works for my brain. I was able to create a lifestyle that is generous and beautiful, and this took a creative approach because my brain is not actually like the brains of about 85 or more percent of the population! In the book "Driven by Distraction" I fit the description of "race car" brain perfectly. If you say one thing to me, I jump ahead about seven sentences and I tap into my intuition and suddenly I get where you are going. So this can be challenging if you don't understand this about me. As I recognized how I work and what works for me, my entire life went into high gear creation and has not stopped for a moment.

I laugh sometimes when people try to argue with me that I could not possibly self-diagnose myself. When you do know something to be true about yourself, what if this is not a wrongness? I stepped into how can this be a rightness, and feeling the rightness of it, for me.

So instead of taking about two years between books, my creativity consciousness came up with one book every month where I would invite people to write and create and generate stories that would change the world. In this way, I am always looking at new ideas, meeting new people, editing and reading new chapters, and learning new stories. If that doesn't spell happy for my brain, I don't know what does!

So when I look at expansion in my life, one of the steps that my life required was to have new awareness of how I function, and then, after that, the more challenging pieces were to put things into place so my focus could be honored and my gifts given space to flourish.

Honoring Your Strengths

As I met for lunch with one of the amazing authors in this book, John Hittler, of EvokingGenius.com, he chatted with me about my annual Happiness Telesummit. I had been dragging my feet about the event, and I had not felt creative or generative. I recalled with joy two years ago when one of my tech savvy colleagues had taken on all the tech pieces, and I was able to focus on the interviews. Joy! That was so much joy!

As I sat with John, I got a clear picture and invited new tech help into the summit for 2015. Slam! The energy shifted and the event became alive. I was able to build a beautiful summit (or that is how it is projecting itself as this book goes to press) and create new forces for love, joy, energy, expansion, healing, happiness and all of the creative genius that shows up in that event. It took recognizing the role that I can play and inviting help for the roles that I am not best and perfect to play.

I laugh sometimes about the concept of expansion, and I laugh to myself because when it shows up it really isn't exactly what I thought it would be. There is more space, and more delicious anticipation because there are more events and more exciting opportunity.

Get the Energy of What You're Seeking

When you can relax on the exact how, the expansion can be in your life with a miraculous immediacy. Here's how I found the perfect car after about five weeks of looking. My last car was totaled in an accident on Halloween, no one was hurt. I was driving a rental vehicle for almost two months, over Christmas, not ready to figure out the kind of car that was perfect for me.

As a mom of three children, a family car made sense, but I was tired of the Yukon XL I used to drive. I drove a Honda Accord for a few months, but it wasn't quite big or safe enough. So I kept going back and forth between Cute (I really like cute cars) and Practical (I don't like practical cars too much) and sexy (I really like sexy cars) and then I followed some of the Access Consciousness® tools on will this car make me money? But what I didn't do was just see the energy of the car that would work for me. This was all coupled with some resistance because I don't care that much about the vehicle at all (any vehicle). It just isn't in my nature to care too much about vehicles.

So I stopped everything one morning when I was about to pay another costly week of a rental vehicle and wrote down what I truly seek. I wrote down safe, seats eight, fuel as efficient as is possible with my big family.

Then I got on the internet and landed on the Mazda local site (I'm still not sure why because I wasn't looking for a Mazda). The Mazda local site had a Honda Pilot for sale (seats eight) and it was calling my name. I decided in that moment I would buy that car that day. When I went in, that car was sold! Oh no! However, a Honda Pilot was available for $1,000 less and it wasn't on the market yet. It had a few scratches. It was about $1K below the Kelley Blue Book value. So I was a big yes and drove it home shortly afterwards.

The whole experience was so easy and fun and wonderful, and I have a vehicle that is easy on gas and fits my whole family with ease. Plus it feels big and safe. I didn't think of that particular car as cute, but so far everyone in my life loves it too (especially the people who matter, my trio of munchkins).

When you let go of exactly what MUST happen and ask questions about what could happen, expansion can show up in ways you just don't even know yet. I get chills when I think about how miraculous life can be!

How Much of You do You Give Your Dream Life Daily?

I love what showed up when I was speaking to a group of eighth graders recently. I asked them to start making a deposit every day on their dreams. I could see in my mind's eye that the only thing standing between me and the dreams I have for me is, me! My actions, my behaviors, and my beliefs can turn into dreams at warp speed.

So, one of the girls wanted to become a writer, and I suggested she write each and every day. Her teacher was also a writer with a beautiful story to tell about a girl and her horse. I encouraged her to draw and paint illustrations, because she does, but had not given herself permission to take the time to illustrate her own story.

A boy was interested in becoming a pro-level athlete. I asked if he could get there by playing video games and hanging out on the couch after school each day. That was funny because the answer was so obvious. His next steps would be to train with intense purpose, but he might have a difficult time getting to his dream if he doesn't take tangible steps. You want to take your dream, and then put a bit of energy each day into it, and keep believing it, and keep investing in yourself to turn it into reality.

Conscious Awareness and Intention

When you shift what you seek, and ask for it in a big way,

you shift your intention, and you shift the actions that then allow your intention to become real. It requires of you that you change what you seek – first. Then once you are clear on what you seek – the very energy of that – then you can invite it in.

Then you have to let go of where you are.

Disabling Reality

This is where sticky gets to go away!

It is vital to disable the hold your current reality has over your life. When you are focused strongly on your current reality, you can actually hold it into place. Your actions and your behaviors are all in alignment with your current reality, so it's really easy to keep it in place. Some of my friends say they have dated the same person in a different body a dozen times, and it never works. So, if you are experiencing the same experience over, and over, and over again – where do you look to change it?

To change reality you can do a few things, and you will most likely need to find your own way to suspend reality and its hold on you. You can begin to shine a light of expansion and invitation on the brightness of one single solitary new experience. Focus on a moment of brilliance and allow that moment to be directly in alignment with the new steps you are taking.

You might not realize where expansion will take you. That

is both thrilling and at the same time challenging. For even as I write this, so many stories in my life have not been written yet. What will happen in my love life next? What will happen for my children and our relationship, next? What will happen to the books and for the books that are presently being written, next?

The questions become wild and unruly sometimes, and the projects and results for me, are getting bigger. I am agreeing to be more, have more, know more, and test myself more.

I find some ugly truths about me where I see what I held into place because I could not let go of something inside of it. Something inside of the sticky felt so normal that releasing it felt really, really strange.

I have been so blessed by the people of this book, and all of their collective journeys, and all of their collective awarenesses. Every day, I awaken to new miracles, and new possibilities. I invite you into the very expansion your being is calling forth.

ABOUT THE AUTHOR: ERICA GLESSING

Erica Glessing is a dreamer, a bright writer, an editor, a publisher, a medium, an animal communicator, a mom, a happiness coach, and a loving spirit.

You can find out more about Erica at www. EricaGlessing.com, www.Facebook.com/ happinessquotations, www.Happiness-Quotations.com, www.HappinessTelesummit.com, and feel free to friend her on Facebook or follow her on Twitter.

Her company, Happy Publishing, is dedicated to publishing the works of light bringers on the planet.

THE END

About Happy Publishing

Happy Publishing is dedicated to supporting authors who wish to change the world. Happy Publishing has published more than 125 authors since its inception. Books released so far include:

The Energy of Happiness (2015)

The Energy of Receiving (2015)

Manifest Change (2014)

The Dreams of Mattie Fitch (2014)

Something About Sophia (2013)

Luxury Home Selling Mastery (2014)

Home Buying Mastery (2013)

Coming up in 2015:

The Energy of Healing (April, 2015)

The Energy of Creativity (May, 2015)

The Energy of Play (June, 2015)

And what else is possible?

Erica Glessing is the CEO of Happy Publishing. Happy Publishing is under Ingram, the finest book distribution company on the planet today.

Erica is a third generation publisher, and second generation published author. She began writing professionally in 1984 as a news reporter. She has written *Prospect When You Are Happy* in 2007 and *Happiness Quotations: Gentle Reminders of Your Preciousness,* in 2011.

She works with writers to bring out the best in them. Happy Publishing was formed with the writer in mind. Email: HappyPublishing@gmail.com.

Happy Publishing

CPSIA information can be obtained at www.ICGtesting.com
Printed in the USA
BVOW02s1255290315

393794BV00014B/443/P